Constructions of Health and Illness
European Perspectives

Edited by

IAN SHAW
School of Sociology and Social Policy
University of Nottingham

KAISA KAUPPINEN
Finnish Institute of Occupational Health
University of Helsinki

ASHGATE

Published by
Ashgate Publishing Limited
Gower House
Croft Road
Aldershot
Hants GU11 3HR
England

Ashgate Publishing Company
Suite 420
101 Cherry Street
Burlington, VT 05401-4405
USA

Ashgate website: http://www.ashgate.com

British Library Cataloguing in Publication Data
Constructions of health and illness: European perspectives
   1.Health - Social aspects - Europe - Congresses 2.Diseases
   - Social aspects - Europe - Congresses 3.Social medicine -
   Congresses
   I.Shaw, Ian II.Kauppinen, Kaisa
   306.4'61'094

Library of Congress Cataloging-in-Publication Data
Constructions of health and illness : European perspectives / edited by Ian Shaw and Kaisa
  Kauppinen.
    p. cm.
  Includes bibliographical references and index.
  ISBN 0-7546-3276-8
   1.Social medicine--Europe--Miscellanea. I.Shaw, Ian, 1957- II.
  Kauppinen, Kaisa.

  RA418.3.E85C66 2003
  610--dc22

                2003065716

ISBN 0 7546 3276 8

Printed and bound by Athenaeum Press, Ltd.,
Gateshead, Tyne & Wear.

Contents

List of Contributors

Judith Allsop	Health Policy Research Unit, De Montfort University, UK
Rob Baggott	Health Policy Research Unit, De Montfort University, UK
Ruby C.M. Chau	Department of Sociological Studies, University of Sheffield, UK
Pru Hobson-West	Institute for the Study of Genetics Bio-risk and Society, University of Nottingham, UK
Kathryn Jones	Department of Public Policy, De Montfort University, UK
Ilka Kangas	Department of Sociology, University of Helsinki, Finland
Kaisa Kauppinen	Department of Psychology, Finnish Institute of Occupational Health, Finland
Sara O'Sullivan	Department of Sociology, University College Dublin, Ireland
Hannele Palosuo	Department of Public Health, University of Helsinki, Finland
Elianne Riska	Department of Sociology, Åbo Akademi University, Finland
Ian Shaw	Department of Sociology and Social Policy, University of Nottingham, UK
Anne Stakelum	Department of Public Health, North Eastern Health Board, Ireland
Louise Woodward	Nottinghamshire Healthcare NHS Trust, UK
Sam W.K. Yu	Division of Social Studies, City University of Hong Kong

List of Figures and Tables

Figures

Tables

Acknowledgements

Thanks are due to Kathryn Nokes, who undertook the preparation of the CRC on this project. Many thanks are also due to both the contributors and Ashgate for being understanding of the unanticipated difficulties that emerged in this particular editorial task.

Introduction

Ian Shaw and Kaisa Kauppinen

The genesis of this edited collection lies in the European Sociological Association's (ESA's) biannual conference in Helsinki in 2001. The editors co-chaired the sessions on the health and illness stream. It was also from that conference that the Medical Sociology and Health Policy Research Network of the ESA finally emerged. The meeting that formed that research network also promoted the idea of an edited collection of papers around the key theme - constructing health and illness. As a consequence, many of the papers in this collection have been developed from presentations made at that conference. However, the editors looked beyond the conference presentations, seeking contributions from other authors in creating a 'balanced' edition that covers the main areas of social construction as it relates to health and illness.

What has become known as the 'constructionist debate' is now one of the most important elements within the sociology of health and illness (Bury, 1996; Nettleton, 2000). This debate arose in the 1960s with Goffman's critique of psychiatry and the role of medical treatment (Goffman, 1961). The resulting discourse helped form the anti-psychiatry movement and the view that psychiatrists were powerful agents of social control (Szasz, 1970). This questioning of diagnostic categories was not limited to psychiatry. In particular, Friedson's work illustrated how diagnosis was mediated by the social and political context in which doctors were practising (Friedson, 1970). Medical belief systems are now seen to be constructed in similar ways to any other belief system (Comaroff, 1982). The examination of doctor's thinking and beliefs continues to form a strong element in contemporary sociology and that is also reflected in this edited collection. In particular in the contribution by Elianne Riska, in her study of the discourse of pathologists, and also in the ways in which rumour may be used to raise issues onto the medical agenda, as in Shaw and Woodward's study.

The 'constructionist debate' was also carried into everyday life. In the main this was due to the works of phenomenology thinkers such as Berger and Luckman (1967). They argued that everyday knowledge is creatively produced by individuals and is orientated around the practical problems of everyday life. Accordingly, to understand beliefs about disease, researchers need to examine and understand the 'common sense' notions of people in society. This has also formed a particularly strong strand in contemporary sociology and again is reflected in this collection. The chapter by O'Sullivan and Stakelum forms a very interesting study of the understandings of an Irish coastal community and the impact that the

Sellafield nuclear power and reprocessing plant has upon their health. Palosuo's chapter illustrates how lay understandings of health can differ in different countries, in this case between people living in Helsinki and Moscow. Chau and Yu's chapter examines the ways in which Chinese people in Britain differentially use Chinese and western medicine and how their understandings of health shape those interactions. Another chapter in this broad theme is the contribution by Kangas. Her study of the changing views of depression and how people account for their own suffering is an insightful contribution to this theme.

A variation on the theme is how lay people operationalise their understandings into resistance and political pressure. This is reflected in Hobson-West's chapter, which focuses upon lay people's resistance to vaccinations. It is also reflected in the contribution of Allsop, Jones and Baggott and their study of health consumer groups in the policy process.

There are now many diverse strands within the constructivist debate in relation to health and illness. One approach is to consider how medical knowledge and facts become socially constructed. Another is to argue that disease entities cannot be divorced from their social context, and research explores how medical science comes to define disease categories. A third would be to look at how social relations are mediated by medical knowledge and medical labelling and this may include how medicine organises itself. A final strand is medicalisation and the way in which medicine comes to make claim over areas previously thought of as 'natural' rather than 'medical'. An example of this is Shaw and Woodward's discussion on the extent to which unhappiness may have been medicalised as depression.

Of course, the critics of constructivist approaches argue that it cannot dismiss a biological reality (Lock, 1988), and the realist approach has recently drawn attention to the limits of constructionism (Bhaskar, 1979; Sayer, 1992). However, constructivism remains a powerful conceptual tool in the critique of the positivist versions of disease that are held by medical professionals. However, there is an increasing awareness that such critiques cannot wholly disregard the materiality of the human body (and mind) and the disturbances to which its biology is subjected (Dingwall, 2001, p.vii). As Dingwall points out, medical sociology has to steer a course between these two pressures. This is also recognised in the papers that form this collection.

We hope that you get as much enjoyment from reading this useful collection as we have had in editing it.

References

Berger, P.L. and Luckman, T. (1967), *The Social Construction of Reality*, London: Penguin Press.

Bhasker, R. (1979), *The Possibility of Naturalism*, Brighton: Harvester.

Bury, M.R. (1986), 'Social Constructionism and Development of Medical Sociology', *Sociology of Health and Illness*, 8: 137-69.

Comaroff, J. (1982), 'Medicine, Symbol and Ideology', in P. Wright and A. Teacher (eds), *The Problem of Medical Knowledge: Examining the Social Construction of Medicine*, Edinburgh: Edinburgh University Press.

Dingwall, R. (2001), *Aspects of Illness* (2nd Edition) Aldershot: Ashgate

Friedson, E. (1970), *The Profession of Medicine: A Study of the Sociology of Applied Knowledge*, New York: Harper Row.

Goffman, E. (1961), *Asylums*, Harmondsworth: Penguin.

Lock, M. (1988), *Biomedicine Examined*, London: Kluwer Academic Publishers.

Nettleton, S. (2000), *The Sociology of Health and Illness* (Reprint and update on 1995 original), Cambridge: Polity Press.

Sayer, A. (1992), *Method in Social Science: A Realist Approach*, London: Routledge.

Szasz, T. (1970), *The Manufacture of Madness*, New York: Harper Row.

Chapter 1

The Work of Pathologists: Visualisation of Disease and Control of Uncertainty

Elianne Riska

Introduction

Most sociological research on physicians' practice has been done on clinical work. As several scholars in the field have observed, sociological in medical work has generally been perceived as residing in the patient-physician relationship, and the rest of medical work has been looked upon as an unpromising area of study since it does not involve any social interaction with the patient (Fox 1992: 11, Atkinson 1995: 34). Strauss et al. (1985) drew attention fifteen years ago to the different kinds of non-patient work going on in a modern hospital, work that they argued deserved sociological study. Part of this work is 'medical production work', which includes, for example, services done at clinical laboratories, where body products, such as blood and urine samples, are examined (Strauss et al. 1985: 53). However, non-patient medical work continues to be an under-researched and under-theorised field within the sociology of professions.

Today, medical production work is a crucial part of medicine. Modern high-tech medicine has created a need for a cadre of research physicians, who never meet a patient but who still have a crucial role in diagnosis. As Conrad (1997, 1999) has suggested, the focus of the medical discourse has narrowed as genetics seems to provide an overall explanation of most chronic diseases. In the age of genetic medicine and molecular biology, the patient has been transformed into a carrier of tissues and genes to be collected for further examination by a variety of medical specialists.

Modernity is a culture that does not accept human mortality except as a problem to be prevented or solved. In modern life, death from natural causes alone is not accepted because, as Bauman (1992: 131) observes, 'death is *the Other* of modern life'. Modernity, as Bauman suggests, has 'killed death', and 'killing of the appointed disease-carriers is a symbolic surrogate of death-killing' (Bauman

1992: 156). The task of defying and rationalising death is in the hands of medical experts. And, as Bauman (1992: 142) notes:

> All deaths have causes, each death has a cause, each particular death has its particular cause. Corpses are cut open, explored, scanned, tested, until *the cause* is found: blood clot, kidney failure, haemorrhage, heart arrest, lung collapse. We do not hear of people dying from mortality. They die of individual causes, they die *because* there *was an individual cause*.

While Foucault (1975) in his exposé of the rise of the new medical gaze of modern medicine portrayed pathology as part of a new regime of science, Bauman (1992) gives pathologists a special task in the deconstruction of mortality in the age of modernity.

The cultural mandate of the pathologists to defy death has the microscope as its instrument. Microscopy of tissue samples constitutes the everyday work done by pathologists. The tissues are treated as objects to be examined or acted upon, and the examination of the disease is totally decontextualised from the patient. The minute details of the properties of tissue samples are further constructed as objects by colouring techniques and by means of a new visualising enhancing computer technology called 'imaging'. This kind of work is also done by haematologists. In his study of a haematology clinic, Atkinson (1995) found that the clinic was the site of a liturgy that involved how to see, name, and describe the blood samples: a special visual and oral culture had been developed by haematologists. The interaction between the haematologists was part of the 'social production of knowledge' going on in the clinic.

The work of pathologists also involves 'medical knowledge production' and 'social production of knowledge'. Pathology is characterised by non-patient work: pathology is a consulting specialty but done generally in a hospital. In the division of medical labour, pathology is a domain structurally isolated from clinical work. The structural separation and the symbolic content of pathology are two traits conducive to the emergence of shared experiences among those working in the field. Work is, for most part, done alone. When the diagnosis entails more ambiguous tissue samples, work is done as teamwork. Aside from the structural identity of being a pathologist, the situational identity related to doing the work can be approached by means of the analytical tools of 'occupational culture' and 'teamwork' provided by Hughes (1958) and Goffman (1959), respectively.

The central aim of this study has been to explore what kind of work a non-patient specialty like pathology entails. This chapter will show that the pathologists describe their expertise as a visual skill - a 'microscopic gaze'. Although 'nature' in the form of the biological raw material of the human body constitutes the objects of their work, subjectivity is projected into these tissues. Humour becomes a way that the pathologists as a collective deal with the emotions in complicated cases, especially since the mandate of the work requires that the tissues be treated as mere matter.

Material and Methods

The material for this chapter derives from a study of the character of work of pathologists. The original inquiry was into why so few women practised in this field in Finland (see Riska 2001), but the study mapped the general character of the work as well. The health care setting in Finland was selected for this study for two reasons. Finland is an interesting case in that, in 1998, half of the members of the medical profession were women. Still, in 2000, only 28 per cent of the pathologists were women, which is one of the lowest percentages outside of surgery (14 per cent) (FMA 2000).

For the purpose of the study, ten of the 46 women pathologists practising in Finland in 1998 were initially selected from the list of pathologists appearing in the official catalogue of *Physicians 1997-1998* issued by the Department of Health and Welfare in Finland. This catalogue lists all licensed physicians in Finland by specialty, by last name in alphabetical order, and by rank and place of work. The women selected for interviews were chosen to represent different age groups, work settings, ranks, and regions of the country. The interviews were conducted from November of 1998 to the beginning of February of 1999. One of the women selected had moved abroad, and so another woman in a similar position was selected, and one woman did not want to be interviewed. Hence, interviews were done with nine women pathologists. Part of this study has been reported elsewhere (Riska, 2001).

From June to October of 2000, nine male pathologists were interviewed. They were selected from the same catalogue from which the women had been selected. The men were chosen to represent different age groups, work settings, ranks, and regions of the country. One of the male pathologists selected had died and another representing the same age and professional status was selected in his stead. All the men selected consented to be interviewed.

The female-and-male-group proved to be sufficiently large, and certain saturation was apparent as the same themes that had emerged in preceding interviews were repeated, and no substantially new information appeared. Each interview was conducted at a time and place convenient for the informant. The interviews lasted on average 40 minutes.

Semi-structured in format, the interviews followed a list of thirteen questions that covered seven main themes: the motives for selecting pathology as a specialisation, the existence of gendered tracks during specialisation, the organisation of work and internal differentiation in pathology, work culture and language, the existence of men's and women's work in pathology, the reasons for the small number of women in the field, and future challenges in the field. The interviews were transcribed verbatim. The main themes were analysed and coded, using an inductive approach (Glaser and Strauss, 1967).

In the excerpts from the interviews reported below the numbers refer to the interviewee in question and the letters W and M stand for a female and male interviewee, respectively.

The Professional Skill: Visualisation of Disease

The work context of most pathologists is the laboratory of the local hospital or the university hospital. The pathologists' work is 'invisible', since they do not meet patients.

Today, only a small fraction of the work involves doing autopsies, although that work was for a long time the master status of the specialty. As Prior (1989: 86) has noted, pathologists revere autopsy as a prime technique of validation and 'biopsy merely replaces the body with the cell as a causal space'. The primary work of pathologists is to examine tissue samples collected as part of routine screening or sent to them by a clinician. After microscopy of the sample, the pathologists send their diagnosis and a written report to the clinician, whose task it is to convey the diagnosis to the patient and make the decision about measures to be taken.

Microscopy requires a visual skill: to be able to see and recognise the patterns of normality and pathology. But this skill is not a mere passive reading of pictures but also a capacity to capture the shapes of the visual images in the microscope.

> Well what should I say [about the skills needed]. Obviously it requires partly that one needs some kind of visual mind. When you look at something then it sticks in some way. (#2M)

> In practice it requires this kind of relevant skill to recognise patterns and to match the visual observations with known facts ... A certain skill to recognise patterns: you can't do this work if you're not able to see the essential patterns ... I think that it's the same thing in radiology, but not necessarily in other specialties. (# 8M)

> I think the most important skill is a good skill to recognise patterns or to see something in a picture. We know there are different types of patterns, either based on hearing or based on touching and so forth. The pathologist's work is like looking at pictures. You have to make out a picture from forms and colours. If you don't have that visual skill, it's rather futile to take up pathology. (#6M)

But the mere visual skill was not enough. A pathologist needed a capacity to fit the visual images into a recognised pattern - a certain visual memory was required:

It's good to have a visual memory since we operate on a visual basis. We see certain patterns in the microscope and then we have to remember that that pattern fits this or that change or tumour, so we that can give the diagnosis. You benefit from having a visual memory, which I definitely have. (#3M)

Well you have to have a good so-called visual memory. That will at least be an advantage because this is a kind of work that you learn by doing and by looking at samples. When you've seen it, then the next time you remember that this is what it was. And then some kind of common-sense skill, so that you can relate the findings to the knowledge you have of the patient. And being sure when you have to be sure but in doubt when the sample is difficult and somehow differs from the normal. And then in a situation in which you are responsible for the samples when the patient is in surgery and you have to give answers that affect the decision about the surgical procedure. Then perhaps a certain cold reasoning so, that you can work under pressure. (#4M)

Well you need this kind of concentration to examine these samples and obviously some kind of visual memory ... because these samples and changes in the tissues and the cells you examine with your eyes, and in a sense you compare in your mind what kind of similar cases you have had before and on the basis of these you then do the diagnosis. (#1M)

There were certain aesthetic values related to this kind of diagnostic work focusing on details - a visual and aesthetic attraction in microscopy. This aspect of the work was mentioned especially by the women as the reason they had selected pathology as a specialisation (Riska, 2001: 107).

In fact, what originally interested me in pathology was that it is so visual. I could see this kind of electromicroscopy pictures of kidneys, and to me it was very exciting and beautiful, and it was this visual side. (# 7W)

Already when I was studying, I realised I saw things in the microscope much better than my fellow students. So in this respect I clearly had a kind of visual memory, and this is visual work. Another thing, certainly, was that when I saw patients at the health center, I always had the sense that I didn't know [the diagnosis] for sure, but if I could open up and see, then I would know. (#9W)

In the women's accounts, the choice of pathology was explicitly or tacitly defended against the normative assumption that their 'natural' choice of future practice of medicine resided in clinical work. Their social and emotional skills, assumed superior to men's, made clinical work with patients the expected, 'normal' thing to do. In contrast, pathology provided an opportunity to explore details and to be concerned with the specifics of diseases, aspects that the women valorised especially. The gender-typing of medical work was so taken for granted that a woman's choice of pathology as a specialisation was still perceived by outsiders as aberrant (Riska, 2001: 108). As a young woman pathologists noted:

I do remember that I was [laughs] leaving the health center to go to try [pathology] out. When I said 'work in the pathology unit', everybody was totally horrified. The women said, 'No, no it can't be true, you can't do that, that's awful'. But I don't understand why only women would be afraid--or I don't know whether it's a matter of being afraid. On the other hand, it might be that women typically are such social beings, they have such social skills for interacting with patients, that they do well on the clinical side [laughs]. They don't have the need to come to the pathology unit to work. Here we don't interact with the patients. (#6W)

For the men, the same aspects were described not as the intellectual challenge and excitement of the specialty but rather in instrumental terms: the research possibilities. A man remembered his motive for becoming a pathologist:

Well, what should I say ... research possibilities, to put it bluntly. Yes, it was it ... research opportunities that influenced me. (# 2M)

And, another man noted,

As a medical student I worked in the anatomy division while I was doing my dissertation. It was rather natural to continue to work in pathology, and I specialised in pathology. (#9M)

The informants considered that the clinical gaze involved with patient work required other skills. Clinical work implies a large patient load in a health centre setting, quick decisions, and no possibility of exploring the science aspects of illnesses. Clinical work is perceived as demanding and characterised by uncertainty because the sick person as a whole, including external social aspects, has to be considered. Most of the time, the diagnosis and the treatment in clinical work had to be done alone in the office or health centre. To the pathologists, the real cause of the disease could generally not be found under such conditions.

As Bauman (1992: 142) notes, unexplained death is a challenge to a world view that deconstructs mortality as a complex web of individual causes. In order to read the body and to reach an 'accurate' diagnosis, the pathologists adhered to what Foucault (1975: 149) has called the 'principle of tissual communication'. The tissues are the carriers of the facts of the disease because the cause of the disease is inscribed in the tissues. This view sees disease as inhabiting the tissues, and a decontextualisation of the body - a tissue under a microscope - will provide the final answer about the cause of the malignancy and the disease. For the informants, the cause and the ultimate truth about disease could be be found in the uninhabited body - the corpse, the organs, the tissues. This required an interest in observing the details of even fragments of organs and tissues.

You have to be interested in hard cases and have patience, so that you can stand to look at these [samples]. Often, the longer you look, the more you find things in them. Often you have to sit for a long time and look, especially in hard cases. Most cases are routine, and those you do fast, but some cases are hard, and then you have to do various types of colouring and additional examinations. And you have to have the endurance to keep looking at them. (#9M)

It suits me that it's this kind of precision work concerned with small details. And then that you can take your time and ponder the problem and not have to make a decision in a horrible hurry, as you have to in clinical work, where you have to make a quick decision whether the patient needs treatment. (#4W)

In sum, a certain visual skill and visual memory were considered to constitute the craft skill of a pathologist. This skill was considered an individual gift and a capacity for doing the work. Routine cases matched the patterns that had been seen before and recognised as fitting the representation. Still a large part of the work was characterised by ambiguity and uncertainty, when the patterns could only be made out after a collective reading. In uncertain cases, when the patterns are ambiguous and hard to define, the reading of the tissue - i.e. the diagnosis - is done as teamwork. Classics in the sociology of the medical profession have suggested that the work of physicians is characterised by uncertainty and that they learn during their training to cope with it (Fox 1957). For the pathologists, uncertainty was a feature of work that did not fit the ethos of the specialty: the task of validating the cause of a disease. The mandate to deconstruct mortality by being experts on the cause of a disease had generated a need for collective work to overcome uncertainty.

The Character of and the Role of Humour in Teamwork

The demands put on the pathologists' diagnoses have increased over the years. Pathologists are no longer merely expected to provide a diagnosis but also to define the gravity and extension of the malignancy. Here is a typical response about the changes in the work:

[Microscopy] looks at increasingly finer details in the tissues and diagnostics. Twenty years ago it was enough to say, 'Yes, this is a malignant tumor'. One did not need to specify further. Today, we have to specify its name precisely, what kind of proteins are on its surface... [Microscopy] has become much more demanding. The clinicians - that is the practicing physicians - know much more and demand that we also give a detailed description of the samples. (#3M)

The demands put on pathology mean that a lot more of what previously were perceived as routine cases now require more work and a more precise diagnosis. In the case of more complicated samples, the individual pathologist consults with other pathologists at the unit, and the final diagnosis is done as teamwork. This feature of collective decision-making and shared responsibility was felt as a special attraction of the work in pathology, as compared to the individual responsibility carried by clinicians. One woman reflected:

> It's nice here in that there are many of us. We show each other the samples. I have this consultation microscope here, and [a woman colleague and I] look together at all difficult samples and get a diagnosis fast. It's nice in this way because two pairs of eyes see better than one.... I like it that you don't have to do [the diagnosis] alone - is it cancer or not, or what is it? (#8W)

A male pathologist saw capacity for teamwork as a basic requirement for good practice:

> It is good if you're social. There's no way that a pathologist can hide in a basement among spiderwebs and bats and vampires and such. You have to be social in the community of pathologists. We consult each other very much, and so you have to be social. You have to be able to communicate with the practising physician because we're consultants. They send us a problem and we try to solve it as best as we can. We give the information back to the clinician, so that he can process it. (#3M)

The pathologists deal routinely with diagnoses that will have or have had mortal consequences for the patient. The taboo-laden character of their work - at least in the eyes of lay people and of many of their colleagues as well - has produced shared emotional experiences in doing the work that can best be expressed by inventing terms that capture their common concerns and constitute their own occupational language. In this sense, both men and women pathologists constitute, in Goffman's terms, a performing team whose occupational language captures the unique features of their work. Their craft is a visual skill that is translated into a shared vocabulary about the character of the tissues as matter and as objects. The informants felt that this language was characterised by the shared human experience of working with material associated with fear of cancer and death. Thus, special words were used to define the situation, to express and manage emotions related to the anxiety of dealing with life-threatening diseases of anonymous patients. The pathologists' occupational language constitutes what Goffman (1959: 142) would have called the inside secret of their teamwork.

> The terminology and this language we use - it differs very much from normal everyday language. And the reason certainly is partly that we deal with very unusual things in our work. This kind of 'Oh, what a wonderful tumour!' or 'Fantastic tumour!' - well, frankly it might sound rather brutal to a lay person. (#2W)

The occupational talk also contained joking that had an emotional and affiliative function, a feature that has been documented in some classics - white-collar workers in bureaucratic organizations (e.g. Blau, 1955: 91-3), Becker et al's (1961) study on medical training, other studies on health care professionals in psychiatric settings (Coser, 1959, 1960), and some more recent studies of health professionals in various health care settings (Yoels and Clair, 1995, Griffiths, 1998, Bolton, 2001). The pathologists had developed a special way of joking to deal with the more strenuous aspects of their work: 'The humour is a little peculiar - this kind of insiders' code and humour' (#8M).

The black humour shared among pathologists was not merely a way of communicating on taboo subjects confronted in work. It also served as a mechanism for coping and for reducing anxiety in dealing with those subjects. Telling jokes was part of the teamwork and served as an integrative mechanism and made the shared tasks tolerable to those sharing them.

> Oh yes at this work place there's a lot of [joking] we laugh a lot. Every day we have a meeting where we go through the interesting or difficult samples that each of us has had. And there we laugh a lot. Partly we laugh at other things, but there's some kind of gallows humour about these samples. Maybe it's perhaps necessary to ease the hardship of everyday life. (#4M)

> We have traditions and then a jargon ... That I'm sure we have. In many ways pathology is hard, a lot of misery and incurable diseases. We make hard diagnoses. So it's obvious that we have to lighten it up and joke a little. But as physicians we respect the patient. Sometimes though, we have to joke about the diagnostics. But we would never say to a patient that we are going to a 'tit' meeting, the breast cancer meeting, just to lighten the language. Sure, there's some jargon, but it has to do with our being physicians. The jargon is there, but we respect the patient, and that is most important. (#3M)

> Pathology is characterised by a kind of black humour because we're doing work relating to death, and then we have to do cancer diagnoses and such things. To relieve the hard work, we joke amongst ourselves rather coarsely, but to outsiders we don't talk that way, we wouldn't want to get a bad reputation. (#3W)

> We do have this horrible kind of joking, but it might partly be due to what's awful. Perhaps it's related to death and corpses. But sometimes you have to be heretical so that you can keep on doing this stuff, it's some kind of mental thing. You get so that [joking] somehow alleviates things. It's not all that nice to dissect corpses or to do an awful cancer diagnosis when you know it's a diagnosis done for some person, it might even be a young person. In some way it [joking] relieves the stress. (#8W)

The black humour in the work of pathologists generally addresses the metaphysical unease about the corpse - its status as materia and as an embodied self (Hafferty, 1988; Young, 1995: 130). Here the very normative basis of pathology is transgressed. In general, pathology's mandate in medicine enters when the body has been classified as matter. The scientific discourse of medicine, including that of pathology, sanitises and abstracts the description of the body. In contrast, the black humour transgresses the high and professional discourse of pathology and introduces the low, the profane, and the grotesque features of the work (see Young, 1995: 130). The humour deals with the ambiguous character of tissues, tissues that are part of living patients who might have a fatal disease. The ambiguity of the status of the tissues has therefore a cultural dimension: the tissues are not mere matter but are also carriers of emotions and caring for the well-being of an anonymous patient.

But in the anatomy labs, in front of the medical students, there prevails a more sombre culture. Only among status equals is joking allowed; in interaction with medical personnel, medical students for example, who are not colleagues, humour is avoided (see Yoels and Clair 1995, Griffiths 1998). In fact, humour might threaten the hierarchical structure of the medical setting in which the supervising physician is teaching the medical students the arts of pathology. As Coser (1960: 85-86) already noted, the status structure is supported by downward humour and too much humorous behaviour on the part of the junior staff might be interpreted as questioning the teacher-student relationship. Similarly, one of the younger women pathologists put down any student joking in the supervised context of dissecting cadavers:

> .I remember when I came here to [the department of] pathology I was surprised how incredibly - how should I describe it? - rigid the procedures and choices of words were about those autopsies and how you were allowed to talk. It was, I mean, you immediately got long glances if ... if you chose some type of even slightly emotional word. They were very strict about it - you were not allowed to use coarse language, even if it was by no means degrading language. Immediately we would be guided and supervised in some way - 'Oh, now you mean this and that'. (#1W)

Conclusion

As Hughes (1958: 54) observed in his classic on the culture of occupations, the work of some occupations routinely deals with emergencies. He noted that such occupations build up devices to help them maintain control over their professional and private life. Pathologists deal routinely with what are emergencies to other people, like confronting the likelihood of cancer.

This study examines the work of pathologists, in particular how they describe their craft skill: visualisation of disease through microscopy. In the view of most outsiders, doing autopsies still forms the master status of the pathologists. However, today the main task of pathologists is microscopy: to provide clinicians with expert opinions about tissue samples from live patients who are screened for, or have had, or will have, surgery for some ailment or disease. The consulting task entails either the confirmation of the normality of samples or the identification of pathology. This information is conveyed to the clinician.

Microscopy requires a 'microscopic gaze' (Atkinson, 1995), a visual skill that enables the pathologist to read the character of the tissue samples. To see, name, and describe the normal or the pathological in the tissue requires a shared knowledge and common concepts. Pathologists have learned and continue to construct in their work a shared representation of what they are visualising. The pathologists' written case reports to the clinicians further reconstruct and confirm the body and organs as representations and as a text. Yet, confirming the normality of tissues of living patients still involves anxiety since most of the plausible pathological signs are sentences of death.

Routine cases are done alone. In routine work the visual evidence is identified and perceived as unproblematic. In the routine cases, the microscopic evidence is compared to a multitude of expected and previously learned and recognised representations. This part of the work is what Atkinson (1995: 78) has called the 'craft skill of recognition'.

When the evidence is not clearly legible, the diagnosis - the degree of certainty contained in the microscopic evidence for making the final decision about the status of the disease - is a result of a working consensus of the team. It is particularly in teamwork that the shared task of identifying the sample becomes part of the 'social production of knowledge'. Teamwork changes the character of the work: the routine backstage work of solitary reading the samples moves to a frontstage, to a social arena. Sharing the reading of the sample with others means that the process of seeing and reading enters the social and becomes 'doing pathology'.

By definition, the difficulty of the reading and identification of the visual signs inherent in the sample concerns more than the mere visual aspects of the sample. The patterns seen in the tissue entail an ambiguity in the status of the tissue as an object and as a subject. The collective reading therefore does not merely address the sample as materia but also addresses the future health status of the patient. The collective task entails the moral dimensions of using the microscopic evidence to interfere in the intimate life of a stranger, an emotional task that transgresses the mandate of pathology. The ambiguity of the patterns and thereby the uncertainty of the diagnosis touches on the taboo-laden emotions and caring for the well-being of an anonymous patient, who still has a mythic presence in the work of the pathologists.

The scientific discourse of medicine sanitises and abstracts the description of the body. This is especially the case with pathology, which treats the body, organs, tissues, and cells as mere matter. The jargon and the humour involved in the teamwork of pathologists generally address the metaphysical unease about the body - its status as materia and as an embodied self. Teamwork is therefore not only a format of work and part of the social production of medical knowledge but it also has an emotional function. To counter the emotions surrounding their work, pathologists have developed their own occupational language and humour, to be able to describe among themselves the work they are doing. The jargon and joking that have emerged in teamwork are collective devices whereby the ambiguity and uncertainty of the status of the sample and of the diagnosis are collectively handled and controlled.

References

Atkinson, P. (1995), *Medical Talk and Medical Work: The Liturgy of the Clinic*, Thousand Oaks, CA: Sage.

Bauman, Z. (1992), *Mortality, Immortality and Other Life Strategies*, Cambridge: Polity Press.

Becker, H.S., Greer, B., Hughes, E.C. and Strauss, A.L. (1961), *Boys in White: Student Culture in Medical School*, Chicago: University of Chicago Press.

Blau, P.M. (1955), *The Dynamics of Bureaucracy: A Study of Interpersonal Relations in Two Government Agencies*, Chicago: University of Chicago Press.

Bolton, S.C. (2001), 'Changing faces: nurses as emotional jugglers', *Sociology of Health and Illness*, 23, 85-100.

Conrad, P. (1997), 'Public eyes and private genes: historical frames, news construction, and social problems', *Social Problems*, 44, 139-54.

Conrad, P. (1999), 'A mirage of genes', *Sociology of Health and Illness*, 21, 228-41.

Coser, R.L. (1959), 'Some social functions of laughter', *Human Relations*, 12, 171-82.

Coser, R.L. (1960) 'Laughter among colleagues', *Psychiatry*, 23, 81-95.

Finnish Medical Association (FMA) (2000), *Physicians in Finland 2000* (Leaflet).

Foucault, M. (1975), *The Birth of the Clinic*, New York: Vintage Books.

Fox, N.J. (1992), *The Social Meaning of Surgery*, Milton Keynes: Open University Press.

Fox, R.C. (1957), in Merton, R.K., Reader, G. and Kendall, P.L. (eds), *The Student-Physician*, Cambridge, MA: Harvard University Press.

Glaser, B.G. and Strauss, A.L. (1967), *The Discovery of Grounded Theory: Strategies for Qualitative Research*, New York: Aldine de Gruyter.

Goffman, E. (1959), *The Presentation of Self in Everyday Life*, New York: Doubleday/Anchor.

Griffiths, L. (1998), 'Humour as resistance to professional dominance in community mental health teams', *Sociology of Health and Illness*, 20, 874-95.

Hafferty, F.W. (1988), 'Cadaver stories and the emotional socialization of medical students', *Journal of Health and Social Behavior*, 29, 344-56.

Hughes, E.C. (1958), *Men and their Work*, Glencoe, Ill.: Free Press.

Prior, L. (1989), *The Social Organisation of Death: Medical Discourse and Social Practices in Belfast*, Basingstoke: Macmillan.

Riska, E. (2001), *Medical Careers and Feminist Agendas: American, Scandinavian, and Russian Women Physicians*, New York: Aldine de Gruyter.

Strauss, A., Fagerhaugh, S., Suczek, B., Wiener, C. (1985), *Social Organization of Medical Work*, Chicago: University of Chicago Press.

Yoels, W.C. and Clair, J.M. (1995), 'Laughter in the clinic: humor as social organization', *Symbolic Interaction*, 18, 39-59.

Young, K. (1995), 'Still life with corpse: management of the grotesque body in medicine', In Young, K. (ed.) *Bodylore*, Knoxville: University of Tennessee Press.

Chapter 2

Constructing Risk: Rumour as a Resource for Medical Sociology

Ian Shaw and Louise Woodward

Background

The genesis of this chapter lies in several newspaper reports in both the *Guardian* and *Times* newspapers and then in the Nottingham local newspaper (the *Evening Post*), during the period January to March of 2000, that GPs were experiencing problems with patients and their use of the Internet. These separate reports varied slightly in content but concurred that patients were arriving at GPs surgeries with sometimes reams of information about their (sometimes-guessed) condition, which had been downloaded from the Internet. These patients were reportedly using this information as the basis of demands for either treatments that the GPs saw as inappropriate or treatments not available on the UK National Health Service (NHS). These reports did not contain any substantial corroborating information but referred mainly to third-hand accounts: i.e. reports from GPs who had heard reports from other colleagues. This raised the question in our minds as to whether such reports had an actual basis in fact or if they constituted some form of urban myth (where GPs say that they know it is widespread but we can find no one who has actually experienced it).

The authors sensitivity to the possibilities of using urban myth or rumour as a basis for analysis in medical sociology was raised by a paper written by a colleague, Robert Dingwall, who used urban myth analysis when relating the case of the 'missing kidney' (Dingwall, 2001). In Dingwall's work, rumours surrounding theft of kidneys from young people after attending nightclubs had a definite moral quality. However, similar work at around the same time by Castaneda (2000) saw child organ stealing stories more in terms of risk surrounding technology. It is clear that neither was aware of the other's work at the time they were writing. In relation to this project, we hypothesised that any 'urban myth/rumour' may also link to the risks that GPs saw emanating from technological development – in this case the Internet. It has long been recognised that technological development and change brings new risks:

> Every technology produces, provokes, programs a specific accident ... The invention of the boat was the invention of shipwrecks. The invention of the steam engine and the locomotive was the invention of derailments. The invention of the highway was the

invention of three hundred cars colliding in five minutes. The invention of the aeroplane was the invention of the plane crash. I believe that from now on, if we wish to continue with technology (and I don't think there will be a Neolitic regression), we must think about the substance and the accident (Virilio, 1983: 32).

However, how does this link to the media reports and the possibility of an urban myth? Does the existence of health information on the Internet lead to the risk of misinformation and inappropriate action or is the risk more one of challenging the doctor's status as 'health knowledge holder'? A small research grant was secured to explore the research questions early in 2002. The funding allowed a small number of interviews (5) with GPs to be conducted. This was then followed by a survey amongst 140 local GPs. GPs were asked, over the period of a month, to note the number of consultations they had that included any discussion from the patient of information on their condition gained from any source outside that of the GPs surgery.

The Interviews

Gaining access to GPs is notoriously difficult. At the time of the research (and at the time of writing) there are very real concerns over a shortage of available GPs, those in training, and those about to retire. GPs lead busy working lives and are not easily persuaded to engage in research unless they have some interest in it. The interviews were short; lasting only between 30-50 minutes and took place over lunch in the GPs surgery. The findings confirmed that those GPs interviewed were aware of the reports and that they gave some credence to them but had little real first-hand experience of the phenomenon.

> Yes, I am aware of colleagues who have experienced difficulty with patients who come into the surgery with prior information, sometimes downloaded from the Internet and which creates problems in the consultation (GP2)

> Patients are becoming more and more informed about their health and illness and less inclined to accept their doctor's judgement as the correct course of action ... particularly if they are seeking a diagnosis that I do not believe is appropriate to them (GP1)

> Patients tend to be more anxious now than in the past. I think this is related to the increasing public awareness of disease and incapacities that can befall them. This is not necessarily a bad thing as they are also probably more likely to look after themselves better (GP4)

However, one GP was of the view that:

> I have read the reports in the press and I am sure that such problems occur. However, in my view a patient who is interested in their health is better than one who is not – and these do exist. (GP5)

Although she went on to say that:

Patients do sometimes come seeking particular forms of treatment, from information gained from magazines or the Internet or wherever. It can sometimes be difficult to convince them that some other remedy or even diagnosis is appropriate (GP5)

In summary the GPs were of the opinion that 'a problem' existed but had varying views on the seriousness or extent of that problem.

The Survey Results

There were 80 individual returns from the survey. This represented GPs from 23 practices, mostly urban in situation, and reflected a 64 per cent response rate.

GPs were first asked to provide information on the number of patients consulting them within the last month. This ranged from 60 to 900. The total number of consultations reported for all the GPs surveyed was 20,535. This left a mean of 419 patients consulting in the previous month. GPs would usually run between 7 and 9 sessions in a week and see around 15 patients per session, so this average figure of 419 is comparable with that level of service and within normal service delivery parameters for the NHS.

Patients gaining information from specific sources

Of all those patients consulting their GPs over the past month, the GPs reported a very small number of people who revealed any 'outside' knowledge source about their symptoms/condition during the consultation. Of the patients that did have prior information they reported that their knowledge was gained explicitly from sources such as books, journals and newspapers, (3.96 per cent of total); 18 patients in total (2.82 per cent) gained knowledge from the television, 4 patients from a support group (0.49 per cent), 15 patients gained knowledge from NHS Direct on-line (1.22 per cent) and, 30 of the sample had revealed knowledge of their condition gained from other internet sources (1.92 per cent). This means that a total of 45 patients from 419 had gained information from the Internet and 15 of them had information directly from the NHS provided website.

Patients consulting NHS Direct on-line

With regard solely to those 15 patients who had gained their additional knowledge about their condition from NHS Direct on-line, 47 per cent of the GPs claimed patients had no more than a normal understanding of the illness and prognosis, 11 per cent of the GPs claimed patients had a worse than average understanding, and 37 per cent of the sample claimed they could not say whether or not patient's understood their prognosis better or worse compared with patients in general.

Thirty-nine per cent of GPs claimed that in reference to patients' knowledge about their treatment options, those with additional information from NHS-Direct appeared to have an average understanding, 11 per cent of GPs claimed patients demonstrated a better than average knowledge, and 17 per cent of the sample suggested their patients had a worse understanding than patients in general. Compared to patients in general, 17 per cent of GPs stated that those patients with additional information gained from NHS Direct on-line had an above average ability to ask the GP appropriate questions; 28 per cent of GPs claimed patients in the past month had only an average ability, 17 per cent of GPs regarded clients as possessing a worse than average ability, and 39 per cent of GPs could not comment. In terms of patients' overall knowledge of their condition, 39 per cent of GPs said patients demonstrated an average knowledge, 11 per cent claimed their patients had above average knowledge, 17 per cent claimed patients demonstrated below average knowledge having gained information from NHS Direct on-line, and 33 per cent of GPs claimed that they could not comment.

Patients consulting other Internet sources

Of those 30 patients consulting 'other internet sources' 41.2 per cent of GPs involved with those patients claimed that they had a better than average knowledge about their prognosis, 24 per cent claimed patients' knowledge was average, 6 per cent worse than average, and 29 per cent GPs could not comment. Forty-seven per cent of the GPs dealing with these patients claimed that compared to patients in general those consulting other internet sources had better than average knowledge about their treatment options, whereas 27 per cent of GPs suggested patients had an average knowledge and only 3 per cent of GPs saw their patients to be below average in their understanding.

Forty-seven per cent of GPs whose patients consulted Internet sources stated that they asked 'appropriate questions', 32 per cent claimed patients had an average ability to ask questions and 18 per cent could not say. Sixty-two per cent of GPs stated that patients who had consulted them in the past month, with additional information from the Internet, had a better than average overall knowledge of their condition in comparison to 3 per cent of GPs who claimed that patients had a worse than average knowledge.

Anxiety level

Forty-three per cent of GPs whose patients had consulted NHS-Direct on-line reported that those patients had an increased level of anxiety compared to patients in general, 4 per cent claimed that patients had showed no sign of change and 4 per cent claimed anxiety had decreased in comparison to patients in general. However, 50 per cent of GPs were unable to say. In comparison to the above, 39 per cent of GPs claimed that patients consulting other internet sources revealed increased levels of anxiety, but 36 per cent claimed patients had shown no difference in anxiety levels. Twenty-one per cent could not say.

Helpfulness in consultation and treatment process

Fifty-four per cent of GPs caring for the 45 patients who had consulted various Internet sources thought that the knowledge gained was helpful for both the patient and the consultation, 26 per cent of GPs stated they were neither helpful nor unhelpful. Only 8 per cent of GPs – 3 GPs dealing with 4 patients in total, claimed that the information that their patient had was unhelpful. Nine per cent had no view.

As a consequence it can be shown that of all the 20,535 patients consulting the GPs in the sample over the previous month less than 0.02 per cent of them had information that the GPs considered unhelpful to the consultation.

Qualitative analysis of open ended questions

In response to a question about the nature of the 45 patients consulting the Internet, five themes emerged from the data concerning whether those patients who had consulted various internet sources share any common conditions, social characteristics or belong to any identifiable social groups. Interestingly, a number of GPs claimed that there was no similarity between patients whatsoever, in stark contrast to those GPs who were divided in their response between what exactly these patients may have in common. A common characteristic suggested by a number of GPs was patients' socio-economic status. It was suggested that patients attending consultation with information from the Internet were from higher social classes, generally middle and upper-middle class. This could be explained in terms of ownership and/or access to a computer and their willingness to challenge GPs authority. Secondly, some GPs claimed that patients tended to be younger or, if older, were more academically able and likely to have consulted the Internet. Further to this, patients with helpful information gained from the Internet were reported to tend generally to be more time consuming in the consultation, which can lead to the GP having problems managing their patient workload.

In summary, the evidence would seem to refute the existence of the problem that was of concern to GPs and was reported in the media. Indeed the analysis suggests that the incidence is so rare that this is very unlikely to be a case of 'frequency anomaly' where several GPs get a lot of such cases over a short time span and report it as a personal event which then gets picked up by others.

Discussion with respect to a myth analysis

Castaneda reminds us that a rumour is a 'story without an author, information without a definite origin, whose truth is always in question' (Castaneda, 2000, p137). If this is the case and it was a myth the question it raises is what risks or moral may underlie it? Risks are viewed as such through the social process of 'problematisation' and sometimes in the absence of empirical evidence on the nature and extent of the actual situation or dangers (McNally, 2000). That fits with the situation in this study. The identification of risk is a social and political process. In this process, some dangers may be identified as risks - and 'floated' on the political agenda as such - but never actually achieve the status of 'risk' in the broader sense. Castaneda is clear that 'rumour is a site in which the play of authorization and de-authorization of risk makes itself especially evident' (Castaneda, 2000: 139). Consequently, the subject of this study may reflect a situation where GP's concerns over the impact of the Internet on patients and/or their relationship with them is seen to pose a risk and the rumour is one way of getting that risk onto the social and political agenda.

Medical concern about the possible adverse effects of information on the Internet upon health is not new. For example, there has been a running debate through the pages of the BMJ since at least 1996, for example in the November 2002 edition, although the very small number of cases involved is now acknowledged. However, why should just one of these concerns move from the professional to the broader 'public' media in early 2000 and portray the problem as significantly larger than it is? What risk may this rumour be actually aimed at addressing?

The Labour Government (since coming to power in 1997) has been keen to 'modernise' public services. This is particularly the case with respect to the NHS, where doctors, nurses and even managers (though valued) were seen to be a part of a traditional culture that was resistant to change. The path towards modernisation was to involve more of the public in the running and evaluation of services. Legislation to involve more of the public in the NHS's work followed. For example, the NHS Plan, released in July of 2000, was one such piece of legislation. Chapter 10 of that plan included a section on 'Information to empower patients' and unveiled its 'expert patient programme'. This programme utilises the Internet to navigate the maze of health information. Patients will be able to use this information to choose their GP. They are also to have more choice in where a referral is made and, from 2005, be able to book the time and date of hospital treatment themselves.

The plan also unveiled new mechanisms for dealing with under and poor performance among individual doctors. Performance checking now includes annual appraisal and 5 yearly revalidation of skills plus mandatory participation in clinical audit. A patients' Forum is to be established in every NHS & Primary Care Trust and there is now an increase in lay representation on regulatory bodies, including the GMC. New and speedy ways of dealing with patient complaints are also under review.

Could the imminent release of this NHS Plan (at the time of the reports) be a cause of the rumours? Certainly, the reporting of the rumour slowed down considerably after its publication. Brunvand (1983) advocates an examination of the *performance* of contemporary legends:

> What little we know about *who* tells the stories, *when* and to *whom*, and *why* invariably contributes to understanding how legends function and what they mean.

One hypothesis could be that doctors (or at least some of them) see the NHS reforms as a threat to their social order or status. Is that why the notion of the '(mis)informed patient' is portrayed as a recipe for disaster? Certainly Beck's work posits a constant and complex struggle between the forces of modernity and those that can be regarded as 'traditional'. Here, each move to modernisation is resisted by a 're-traditionalisation' in response to the risks involved in the modernisation process (Beck, 1992).

Just as Kornhauser (1960) and Morin (1971), explored the ways in which bourgeois elite saw industrialisation and urbanisation as jeopardising their role as responsible and benevolent leaders of the less fortunate and less gifted. Could this rumour be analysed in similar terms with the doctors in the role of bourgeois and the patient as the 'less gifted', but with the informed patient rather than industrialisation being the challenge?

What in positive terms could doctors gain by the spread of such a rumour (Strong, 1990, 1998)? And how might this help define or reaffirm group membership and solidarity?

A better way of understanding the performance use of myths and so on may be to see them as building blocks of everyday life, something that can be used locally to talk social order into existence (Gubrium, 1989). Rumour is what happens when there is a coincidence of challenges to that order. To the extent to which the story happens to solve or rationalise the problem for those affected, it is likely differentially to be adopted and to be reinforced in transmission.

Brunvand (1983) identified three main elements to myths and contemporary legends: the first is a strong story line, the second is a foundation in actual belief and the third is a popular moral. Morin further argues that rumour should also be seen as a protest against modernity; in this instance the Internet and consumerism form the avant-garde. The Internet is used, and is perceived as a source of innovation and social change. It is also symbolic of a shift in the social order, where the receptacle of knowledge on health and illness is no longer only the Doctor, but also the Internet. This may also be seen as a part of the shift away from the respect doctors traditionally commanded because of their superior learning. The Internet then could be seen to be indicative of structural breakdown, not only of the doctor-patient relationship but also of society itself. The story gains credence and is retold as a protest against modernity.

As Everett Hughes (1971) pointed out, medicine is a keeper of the 'guilty knowledge' that many of the things that we treat as stable, predictable and reliable conditions for action are actually uncertain, insecure and contingent. Doctors are the successors of priests, witches and shamans whose work seeks to manage those mysterious forces that threaten to destabilise everyday life. The general public do not share in this knowledge. Rumours could provide an informal means by which the laity can control professionals – by rumour about their manner, expertise etc. Such rumours may impact upon the sorts of patient a particular doctor sees and consequently his work. It may, however, be possible to analyse them for other purposes. It may be the case that rumour reinforces professional solidarity in times of perceived threat and at the same time makes the public aware that 'doctors know best' despite government policies towards the 'expert' patient.

The clinician feels that his work is unique and concrete, and not really assessable by... anyone who does not share with him that first-hand experience. And he emphasises his own personal responsibility. On both grounds he asserts his autonomy (Friedson, 1970, p. 180).

This also has an impact upon the doctors' professional self-image – those in the profession do not want the principle of caveat emptor to apply to them. They do not want the client to make an individual judgement about the competence of practitioners or the quality of their service. The interaction between professional and client is such that the professionals strive to keep all serious judgements about competence within the circle of recognised colleagues (Hughes, 1971, p.361). The professional registration system ascribes competence to the profession rather than the laity. Thus, the public is protected from its own incompetence, from its own impossible demands, and that the quacks who might exploit them will not be allowed to practice.

Wilson also discussed the traditional notion of the doctor-patient role – the physician as expert and the patient as amateur:

> Possession of the initiative and of recognised competence imply power, they also imply a correlatively heavy burden of responsibility. Although the patient too has important obligations – especially the central one expressed by Parsons as 'to try to get well' – it is the practitioner who must act. He is hourly engaged in what is probably the most difficult of human tasks – decision making – and in a setting where the consequences of error are quite often irreversible and very dangerous. Entrusted with the most precious of assets, the living body and mind, the practitioner must chart a course of therapy... All practitioners are professionals and all patients are amateurs (Wilson, 1963, p. 280)

Contrast this view with current UK government policy on the 'expert patient'. *The Expert Patient – a New Approach to Chronic Disease Management for the 21st Century*, was published in September 2001 (but was under consultation at the time of the rumours in early 2000). This policy document set out how the Expert Patients Programme (EPP) would aim to empower those living with chronic long-term health conditions to become key decision-makers in their own care. It initiated action over a six year period (2001-07) to embed in the National Health Service a lay-led self-management training programme for patients with chronic conditions. Earlier research by Macintyre and Oldman (1977) has relevance to this programme. They also pointed to change in power relationships that the EPP is likely to encounter:

> In claiming that we have become experts in the handling of our migraines we are suggesting that while our knowledge may be gleaned largely from medical sources it is superior to that of individual doctors. This leads to important consequences for the relationship between patient and doctor... While the sufferer may feel his own knowledge to be superior to that of his doctor, the latter may well feel his knowledge to be superior in being more 'scientific' and abstracted from imprecise accounts of many case histories. Our assumed expertise is also a challenge to the doctors' role and his authority of expertise (Macintyre and Oldman, 1977, p.69).

The Expert Patients Programme is effectively about challenging the doctors' control over medication, treatment and consequently their role as gatekeepers to accessing health care resources.

As mentioned earlier, the Expert Patients Programme forms just one part of a wider strategy to make doctors more accountable to lay people, and using information gained from the Internet as a means of doing so.

Everett C. Hughes (1971) in *The Sociological Eye* used the example of a jazz musician to illustrate ways in which musicians keep social barriers between themselves and their audience.

> The musician wants his music to be appreciated, but to have his living depend upon the appreciation does not entirely please him. For he likes to think of himself and other musicians the best judges of his playing. To play what pleases the audience – the paying customers, who are not, in his opinion, good judges – is a source of annoyance. It is not merely that the listeners having poor taste demand he play music which he does not think the best he can do; even when they admire him for playing in his own sweet way, he does not like it, for then they are getting too close – they are impinging on his private world too much. Musicians accordingly use all sorts of little devices to keep a line drawn between themselves and the audience... to create distance (Hughes, 1971: 346)

The question is whether this is analogous to the situation of GPs and the 'informed' patient. Are patients perceived as 'getting too close' and is rumour one of the 'little devices' used to draw the line between themselves and their patients? Certainly Everett Hughes argued that 'part of the social psychological process of the occupation is maintenance of a certain distance from those people most intimately concerned with ones work' (Hughes, 1971: 345).

Perhaps this was an example of what Gubrium terms 'confusion escaped': Gubrium argues that the interpretation of whatever is considered to be troublesome varies with organisational rhythms, but there is a perceived need to do something about the trouble. One way to deal with this, he argues, is to make them go away – to transform troubles by altering their defining context. Moving the emphasis from public concerns about doctors to one more about doctors concerns about patients:

> A better way of understanding the performative use of legends, myths, tales and so on, whether as a collective action or as individual events may be to see them as building blocks of everyday life, something which can be locally used to talk a social order into existence. Their relatively enduring quality may simply derive from the imperturbability of the mundane world... the notion that there is something distinctive about contemporary legends simply reflects the extent to which we have beguiled ourselves with the idea that the modern world is a very different place to its predecessors... Rumour is simply what happens when there is a coincidence of challenges to the social order. To the extent that a particular story happens to solve the problem for those affected, it is likely differentially to be adopted and, once selected, to be reinforced in transmission (Dingwall, 2001: 194-5).

In his study of the missing kidney rumour Dingwall makes the suggestion that rumours may be analysable as a lay means to informally regulate doctors. This study goes further to indicate that rumour may also be used by doctors to informally try to construct risk, perhaps to influence policy or at least to show solidarity at a time of uncertainty and change.

References

Beck, U. (1992), *Risk Society: Towards a New Modernity*, London: Sage.
Brunvand, J.H. (1983), *The Vanishing Hitchhiker: UrbanLlegends and their Meanings*, London: Picador.
Castaneda, C. (2000), 'Child Organ Stealing: Risk, Rumour and Reproductive Technologies', pp. 136-154 in Adam B., Beck U. and Van Loon, J., *The Risk Society and Beyond: Critical Issues for Social Theory*, London: Sage.
Dingwall, R. (2001), 'Contemporary legends, rumours and collective behaviour: some neglected resources for sociology?', *Sociology of Health and Illness*, vol. 23 No. 2: 180-202.
Friedson, E. (1970), *Profession of Medicine*, Chicago: University of Chicago Press.
Gubrium, J.F. (1989), 'Local Cultures and Service Policy', in Gubrium J.F. and Silverman D. (eds), *The Politics of Field Research: Sociology Beyond Enlightenment*, London: Sage.
Hughes, E.C. (1971), *The Sociological Eye: Selected Papers on Work, Self and the Study of Society*, Chicago: Aldine-Atherton.
Korhhauser, W. (1960), *The Politics of Mass Society*, London: Routledge and Kegan Paul.
Macintyre, S. and Oldman, D. (1977), 'Coping with Migrane', in David A. and Horobin G., *Medical Encounters: The Experience of Illness and Treatment*, London: Croon Helm.
McNally, R. (2000), 'Strategic Use of 'Risk' in Gene Technology: The European Rabies Eradication Programme', pp. 112-118 in Adam B., Beck U. and Van Loon, J., *The Risk Society and Beyond: Critical Issues for Social Theory*, London: Sage.
Morin, E. (1971), *Rumour in New Orleans*, New York: Pantheon.
Strong, P.M. (1990), 'Epidemic Psychology: a Model', *Sociology of Health and Illness*, 12: 249-259.
Strong, P.M. (1998), 'The Pestilential Apocalypse: Modern, Postmodern and Early Modern Observations', in Barbour R.S. and Huby G. (eds), *Meddling with Mythology: AIDS and the Social Construction of Knowledge*, London: Routledge.
Virilio, P. (1983), *Pure War*, New York: Semiotext.
Wilson, R.N. (1963), 'Patient-Practitioner Relationships', in Freeman, H.E., Levine, S. and Reeder, L.G. (eds), Handbook of Medical Sociology, Englewood Cliffs, N.J: Prentice-Hall.

Chapter 3

Lay Understandings of Health:
A Qualitative Study

Sara O'Sullivan and Anne Stakelum

Introduction

The North Eastern Health Board (NEHB) region covers the counties of Louth, Meath, Cavan and Monaghan. This area covers a total of 6,498 square kilometres and has a population of 300,183. Geographically, the region extends from the Fermanagh and Armagh borders in the north to the north Dublin boundary in the south. Census data for 1996 (the most recent census data available) puts the population of Co Louth at 92,166, the second largest in the region after Co Meath at 109,732. In terms of population density however, Louth demonstrates the highest population density of 110 persons per square kilometre, with two thirds of this population living in urban areas. In terms of material deprivation 60.7 per cent of the population live in what are classified as deprived district electoral divisions.[1] In addition, within the NEHB counties Co. Louth had the highest proportion of persons living in local authority housing (10.7 per cent) and the highest proportion of persons receiving medical cards (47.2 per cent) which are issued subject to a means test, and entitle the bearer to free medical care.

In terms of mortality, County Louth has continually shown a worse mortality profile in relation to respiratory diseases, cancers (especially lung cancers), and accidents to other areas nationally (NEHB, 2000). North Eastern Health Board figures show that more men from Co. Louth died of lung cancer between 1991 and 1995 than anywhere else in the State. Another study examining deaths in the Republic from 1971 to 1991 found that 'Louth is the worst for lung cancer and is very close to the top for most forms of cancer' (*Irish Times*, 10/9/97).

Residents in Louth have repeatedly expressed concerns that radiation-induced cancers and congenital abnormalities may be attributable to the proximity of the Sellafield Nuclear Plant in the UK (Keogh, 2000). Sellafield is an important issue at the national level in Ireland. All the main political parties now support calls for its closure. The issue also has resonance at the popular level, as evidenced by the recent *Shut Sellafield* postcard campaign, which involved the delivery of over 1.3 million postcards, signed by Irish citizens, demanding the closure of the Sellafield nuclear plant (26th April 2002) to Tony Blair, Prince Charles and British Nuclear Fuel's chief executive. Since 11th September 2002 concerns about the safety of Sellafield have been augmented by fear of a terrorist attack on the plant.

It is a central local issue in County Louth. Members of the *Cooley Environmental and Health Group* have been very critical of attempts to minimise the Sellafield effect. The Director of the Cancer Registry in Ireland has come under particular criticism for attributing high cancer levels in Louth to smoking ('Director of Cancer Registry blames Lifestyle of Louth People for Cancer Deaths', *An Phoblacht*, 11/3/99). A number of local groups have been involved in campaigns against the nuclear reprocessing plant. Four local residents in conjunction with the Irish government took legal action in the British courts aimed at closing the BNFL-operated THORP reprocessing plant at Sellafield (*Irish Times*, 01/02/02). There have also been numerous calls for research into the Sellafield effect (see for example *The Irish Times*, 10/9/97; *The Irish Times*, 16/10/97). In this context it might be expected that popular wisdom might link the high mortality rates in Louth to the proximity of Louth to Sellafield (see also Balshem, 1991: 154).

In order to address these issues, an extensive multi-dimensional study was undertaken of which this study forms a part. The Louth Project explored correlations between mortality profiles and socio-economic variables, incidents of radiation-linked cancers and congenital anomalies, and key lifestyle components in the region. The aim of the qualitative study was to understand commonly held beliefs about health and how these impacted on lifestyle practices across different age groups and genders located in the lower to middle income groups in Co Louth. In this respect it was a response to an identified need for qualitative work to explore findings from quantitative work on lifestyle and health-related issues previously identified (Friel and Kellegher, 1999).

Previous studies of lay health beliefs have demonstrated that it is essential to recognise that lay people have their own valid interpretation of what being healthy means (see for example McCluskey, 1997). These beliefs are not just diluted versions of medical knowledge, but rather are rooted in social and historical contexts. The same biological phenomena can be interpreted differently in different times and places for social and cultural reasons, and these variations in interpretation can lead to different responses and actions. In other words, definitions of health, and accepted ways of producing, maintaining and restoring health are socially constructed. Using this framework, the present study strives to look beyond individual lifestyle choices by focusing on the social meaning attached to these choices.

Participants and Methods

Given the aims and objectives of this study, the use of focus groups was deemed to be the most appropriate strategy for data collection. Focus groups can be defined as the explicit use of group interaction to produce data and insights that would be less accessible without the interaction found in a group (Stewart, 1990). Nineteen focus groups involving 131 lower and middle income participants were undertaken between December 1999 and February 2000. The majority of respondents were recruited using the General Medical Services database [GMS], which consists of all those eligible for medical cards in the county. Letters of invitation plus a consent form and FREEPOST envelope were sent out to 760 people. Previous experience of conducting qualitative health research in the region led us to over-recruit substantially, thus we invited five times the number of participants required for each group. This is in comparison to the focus group literature where it is suggested that you over-recruit by 25 per cent (Krueger, 1988). Young males were found to be the most difficult group to recruit. Our sample consisted of all those who returned the consent form and can be described as a self-selected sample. In addition two Traveller groups were recruited with the help of a primary health care worker.

In keeping with the principles of maximum variation sampling, groups were stratified on the basis of age, gender and geography so as to explore diversity. There were ten female and nine male groups; twelve were drawn from urban settings and seven from rural. Four of the rural groups took place in the Cooley peninsula where the Sellafield effect was expected to be the strongest. All focus groups were held in venues that were local, neutral and convenient. A payment of £20 was given to participants to cover expenses.

Discussions were guided by means of a topic guide, which was specifically designed so as to minimize the potential for participants repeating 'approved' messages about health. This guide was later tested by means of a pilot study, which affirmed that the original design was acceptable, in that it allowed participants to discuss their beliefs about health 'actively and easily' (see Morgan, 1998: 23). All focus group discussions lasted 1-1½ hours and were taped with the participants' permission, and later transcribed verbatim.

Each facilitator wrote detailed memos immediately after the focus group took place, which were then emailed to the other researcher. In the memos, themes and topics were noted, and interpretative work was begun. Data were analysed using NUD*IST 4. This package proved particularly useful for coding, and retrieving coded data. Emerging themes were identified from the transcripts and memos. The researchers used these to develop a coding scheme. This scheme was data driven and largely inductive in nature. Subsequent coding was done by each researcher independently, with regular checking of material in order to ensure inter-coder reliability. New codes were created right up until the end of the coding process. Following Catterall and MacLaran (1997), transcripts were coded on screen for content and off-screen for process. This was to avoid missing contradictions in participants' comments, changes in participant's views etc. In addition, NUD*IST's text search facility allowed the researchers to check hunches and do retrospective coding.

Overview of Findings

A number of key findings emerged from this study, each of which will be presented in turn. Lay definitions of health challenge the notion of health as a unitary concept. Instead, health emerges as complex, multidimensional and dynamic, and respondents were found to have developed a subjective and experiential understanding of health. In the next section we present an overview of this new model for understanding health.

Secondly, the evidence of this study suggests that the 'self-responsible' lessons of health promotion appear to have been widely accepted, as reflected in the absence of a fatalist orientation in lay understandings of health. However, it is important to note that self-control does not occur in a vacuum but is a response to external triggers. This has implications for health promotion initiatives, as we shall see. In addition, it was found that the lay understanding of cancer linked it to environmental factors primarily, while heart disease was related to lifestyle factors.

Finally, it was found that the probability model of risk may prove to be a limited tool in evaluating lay risk as it fails to recognise that both risk and risk assessment are cultural phenomena, intricately bound up in subjective value systems. From this study it is apparent that people accept risks either because they enjoy them or because they believe intuitively or calculatively that, on balance, the expected benefits outweigh the possible costs. Dismissing lay risk assessments as erroneous or unscientific hinders understanding. In addition, an over-concentration on a probability risk model excludes this lay perspective and thus prevents a true understanding of 'risky' behaviour.

Health: Towards a New Model of Understanding.

While there is a tendency among health professionals to view health as a unitary concept, lay respondents in contrast hold complex and sophisticated theories of health. From a lay perspective, health emerges as multidimensional, dynamic and relative, a point also noted in the only previous published Irish study of lay health beliefs (McCluskey, 1989). Here, health was defined along four major orientations.

- Performance orientation: the ability to work and carry out normal roles and tasks.
- Fitness orientation: experience of being active and physically fit.
- Feeling-state orientation: a general feeling of well being.
- Symptom-free orientation: the absence of symptoms or illness.

While all these orientations were also found in this study, other nuances also emerged.

For some respondents, definitions of health were bound up with visiting or avoiding the doctor. Some respondents felt that health is 'about not going to the doctor for starters'; for older people the converse was in fact true. For these respondents their health was something that could only be determined by a visit to the doctor.

> I think if you go to the doctor and you get a clear answer from him that there's nothing wrong, well then you can say you're healthy, but if you don't go to the doctor then you don't know you are healthy.

Here we see respondents drawing on what Tucker (1997) terms the biomedical 'folk' model where health is equated with medicine, and dependent on doctors and drugs. Health was also defined as the absence of illness in many groups. However many of those with illnesses still claim health, so a contradiction can be identified here. This might be how health is defined in general terms, but when respondents spoke about their own health a more subjective definition of health was seen to emerge. Respondents saw health as a subjective and experiential phenomenon.

Health as Relative: '... Everyone is Totally Different'

When participants shifted from objective definitions to more subjective definitions of health, the notion of health as a relative concept emerged. Standards of health are not static but are influenced by stages in the lifecycle, life events, and respondents' own health history. For many, health was a matter of degree rather than an absolute. 'I would not say that I'm not healthy, I'm healthy to a degree' or as another respondent put it 'I'm healthy with a question mark'. This finding is similar to the notion of less than perfect health introduced by Twaddle and Hessler (1977), who argue that there is a range of less than perfect health within which a person is still considered healthy.

The idea of health as a relative concept, while most important in the older groups, was not exclusive to them. A number of different nuances emerged in this regard. Firstly there was the connection made between health status and age. As one respondent put it 'one certainty is the older you get the less healthy you get'. Illness was seen as inevitable as you got older. However, there was also resistance to this equation of ill health and old age, in the sense that aging can affect people differently; 'you can have people of 80 and they are healthy and you can have people of 50 and they are old long before their time'.

Many respondents equated youth with health. There was a feeling that you could do things when you were younger, e.g. smoking and drinking, without damaging your health. It was as if the younger body had a reserve of youth that acted as a barrier to ill health. For younger people, health involved thresholds prior to which health was taken for granted; 'When you hit 50 then you start thinking about it [health]'. One respondent suggests the reason health is taken for granted until a certain age threshold is because it is not threatened. In other words it is illness that concentrates the mind on health. For others it was not illness per se, but rather the fact that as you get older you become aware of your own mortality; 'It's only now [at 40] that you start thinking I have to be healthy, I want to live a good life and live a bit longer'.

Health was also seen as relative to respondents own health history. For some respondents in older groups, health problems were seen as normal. Many argued they were healthy despite having various illnesses and conditions; 'Even though I have me arthritis and that I don't feel down with it because I have lived with it now'. It is as if older participants often expected health problems because of their age and therefore discounted them because of this expectation. This ties in with Fry (2000) who argues that 'older people report surprisingly high levels of well-being' and that well being ratings do not decline according to age.

Respondents were also willing to accept that you can be 'sick but healthy'. However they did make the distinction between 'conditions' and other illnesses. Conditions such as arthritis and diabetes are chronic illnesses that can be managed and so allow you to claim health. Other illnesses disallow you from claiming health, e.g. cancer. Cancer even if it was 'under control' was almost always seen as anathema to health.

Health as Minimal and Maximal Standard: A Paradox

Another lay model for understanding health is the idea of minimal standard, which refers to the notion that you are healthy when you meet or exceed a self-imposed minimal standard -.as one respondent put it 'the normal things in life if you are able to do them then you are healthy'. While the notion of a minimal standard was more prevalent among older respondents, in the younger groups the emphasis was on health as a maximum standard or as an ideal type.

/: Someone who is [healthy is] pretty active, yeah [(ok)], looks after their body, knows what they're eating (right)], eats the right food [(right)]…
/: Unlike us, probably [all laugh].

Related to this is the notion of aspirational health, with young people mainly wishing to do better in relation to their health.

A difference can be identified between older and younger groups in relation to lay definitions. Older groups seemed to want to claim good health, or fairly good health even in the face of illnesses. Younger people and some middle aged people in contrast seemed reluctant to claim health despite the absence of illness. Our hypothesis is that older respondents have developed a personal definition of health over the years as a result of illness. Their definitions of what it is to be healthy are more complex and tend to focus on the minutiae or the everyday. In contrast younger participants have internalised the healthist discourse of health promotion, which leads them to view health in absolutist terms thus rendering it elusive.

Health as Moral Imperative

In recent years, there has been an ideological shift in medical discourse from curative to preventative medicine, resulting in increasing stress being laid on the role of the individual in maintaining his/her health. One consequence of this shift is that moral judgements overlay the attainment of health (Crawford, 1984). Health is understood as a moral imperative. People 'admire' others who look after themselves. Respondents were found to be harsh about those who do unhealthy things, in particular smoking; 'They are neglecting their health that is a fact'. Non-smokers were found to be more likely to minimise the effort required to give up smoking, and to be judgmental about those who cannot give up. Excess drinking was also mentioned by respondents, but was not judged as harshly as smoking. Some respondents also made moral judgements about those who were overweight; 'I think overweight is terrible … it is a terrible burden on people, you could be much more active'.

Our respondents felt the need to apologise or to justify aspects of their lives that they thought unhealthy (see also Backett, 1992: 261). The regular appearance of terms such as 'should' and 'blame' in the transcripts are reflective of this. There was a form of self-flagellation evident in young women's talk about their health behaviour. Terms like 'I'm a disaster' and 'I'm terrible' were used in relation to diet. Note here that it is not the diet that is judged to be terrible, but the self. One respondent described herself as 'the most UNHEALTHIEST PERSON EVER', another said 'I'm very bad'.

The findings of this study indicate that not only was healthiness defined on moralistic grounds, which involved judgements about 'good' and 'bad' behaviours, but it also seemed to slip over into judgements about 'good' and bad' individuals. These judgements were applied both to the self and to others and reinforces the notion of lay health moralities.

Gender and Health

Gender also emerged as an important factor in relation to lay health understanding (see also Saltonstall, 1993). Women were more likely to talk about weight than men were and were more likely to define health in relation to appearance. Men tended to only speak about weight in relation to themselves if they were overweight. Discourse surrounding 'dieting', 'trying to lose weight' or 'feeling guilty' because of over indulgence in 'bad food' were mainly confined to female groups. In contrast, men spoke about eating 'well' or 'properly'. Also self-flagellation was a gendered phenomenon as we have already seen.

Another difference that emerged was in relation to exercise. Young men in particular spoke about exercise as a means to achieving fitness, stressing the physical benefits of exercise; 'I go to the gym to be fit'. In contrast women stressed the mental and social benefits and saw exercise more as a means of weight control than as a means of keeping fit; 'I love going to the gym, it's getting out as well and you know I feel better and I feel slimmer and I feel that I must be losing weight'.

These differences can be seen as reflecting men and women's different relationships to food and the body. These relationships in turn reflect gender norms, which equate slimness and health in women. These findings challenge the medical notion of there being one body differentiated only by biology. It might be suggested that health promotion initiatives in the future be cognisant of this gendered body.

Re-Assessing Fatalism in Health

Respondents in this study were found to have developed a complex understanding of who or what was responsible for health. Health is understood as involving an interplay between external forces and the self. There was no group where the emphasis leaned exclusively in one direction or the other. There was little evidence of a fatalistic orientation and there was a belief across the groups that 'you have a responsibility for your own health'. There was a feeling that in order to achieve health 'it is up to you to look after yourself'. In their talk about health these working-class respondents are making claims to 'moral equality even in the face of clear economic inequality' (Blaxter, 1997: 754).

The evidence of this study indicates that health promotion messages about food, exercise and smoking are generally accepted even if they do not lead to changes in health behaviour. There was a belief in the power of self to control events, and in particular a belief in the potential power of self if you do everything you 'should'. Bordo (1992) has identified a discourse about the body that insists 'on the possibility of creative self-fashioning'. This discourse of possibility means that although 'being healthy' involves a strict exercise regime and diet, it is taken for granted that we should discipline our bodies in this way as the results will be worth it. A belief in the possibility of creative self-fashioning was found across the groups.

> /:There is loads of things you can do [in relation to your health] if you want to do it.
> /: Put your mind to it like.
> /: Will power isn't it.

Despite this belief, very few respondents reported disciplining themselves in this way and the role of the self also involves people choosing unhealthy behaviours.

However, it was found that in those instances where respondents reported embarking on a strategy of self-control, it was typically exercised as a result of external forces. In this instance these relate to:
(a) 'The fright', refers to diagnosis and/or experience of what was perceived as a life threatening illness by the participants themselves;

(b) The vicarious fright: in contrast refers to illness and/or death among friends and close relatives (see also Meiller et al., 1996).

The Fright: 'You wait till you get a problem first and then do something isn't it?'

There was evidence of an unwillingness to take responsibility for own health until you were pushed to do so; changes in diet, weight loss and smoking were all stimulated 'by the fright'. This phenomenon was mainly confined to middle aged and older groups, probably because younger people have not yet really experienced 'the fright'. The evidence of this study would therefore suggest that youth denies young people the 'fright' as a precipitating factor to positive changes in health behaviour. The feeling of invulnerability associated with youth inoculates the young from interpreting a negative experience as a fright.

Some people were found to respond badly to being told by others what to do, but will respond to the fright.

> You wait till you get a problem first and then do something isn't it? Like the way if you feel great like you're keep the way you are you know what I mean [(yeah, yeah)]

> [If] The doctor came up to you and told you you've to give up the fags, well fuck you I'm not giving up fags you know what I mean [(yeah)], it depends if you get a bad fright or bury someone then you will go off them you know what I mean like [(yeah)]... They work better on frights don't they.

The vicarious fright: 'I got a fright when my husband died'

The vicarious fright emerged as another strong theme. While this was not confined to any one age or gender group, it was more common in older and middle age groups. Heart disease emerged as an integral part of the 'vicarious fright'. For some respondents the 'vicarious fright' was a more effective cue to positive health behaviour than advice given by the doctor. Unlike the fright, the 'vicarious fright' has a preventative health component to it. The vicarious fright causes people to take stock before they become seriously ill. However, it must be noted that is not clear whether the change in health behaviour is transitory or long term.

> I got a fright when my husband died, and I wouldn't do the things I did when he was alive, I wouldn't do them now ... I'd be afraid I'd get sick. That frightened the life out of me ... I don't smoke, I don't even drink since he died ... I go to the doctors more often.

> I met him [my neighbour] in the waiting room, he smoked a pipe, he was that failed that I didn't know him, he was dead in a fortnight. I had had a chat about this at home then ... and I said Gabby [wife] do you know I was sitting on death row there today and I said it [apologised for using swear word] I said well fuck it, I said it's going to be me or the fags ... and I just cut them out and that was it.

The results of the study suggest that some of the most important cues to action revolve around social networks and the experience of illness either directly or vicariously, rather than as a result of health promoting initiatives. This is not to say that health promotion education is lost on individuals but rather it is activated only when it is perceived as relevant (Meiller et al.; 1996). The findings suggest that negative changes or a crisis in a person's life can open up possibilities for positive health-related changes. There is a tradition in health education of focussing directly on changing health habits but, as the study suggests, changes in health habits maybe a consequence of changes in a person's life which are social rather than health specific. Health educators in the future might be better advised to put some energy into detecting and harnessing life changes, which act as 'cues' to action rather than just focusing on measuring health outcomes.

Health as Release: The Value of Immediate Enjoyment

While a shift towards individualism has increased the notion of health as a form of self-control, paradoxically it has also created the notion that 'life is for living' and that pleasure should also form part of modern lifestyles. It is apparent from the transcripts that the respondents find themselves astride two opposing mandates, one calling for 'self-control', the other for 'release'. Both mandates are internalised in varying degrees and are variously applied depending on the person and the social context. While some respondents admitted that their health behaviour is governed more by 'release' than 'self-control', most admit that striving for balance is the best option. Health involves a continued struggle between indulgence and denial.

Release, as one respondent put it, 'is about doing what you feel like doing, not what you know you should do'. Release is the antithesis of a regime of self-discipline, denial and self-monitoring. The argument running through the discourse on release is that letting go can make you happy and therefore it can only be good for your health. Release involves enjoyment and allowing yourself the things that you love. Respondents pointed to the pleasure of release; 'I would take cream every day, I'd eat a pound of sweets a day ... I would also take the fat on a rasher, and fat on a chop, I would love it ... I just love it'.

While there were a number of participants who advocated a constant state of release, for the majority health behaviour involves tension between control and release. The evidence of this study suggests that self-control is something that occurs sporadically, and often as a response to a trigger. However 'bad habits' have a tendency to reoccur and self-control is something that is transient for many. Self-control is often followed by release. Respondents fluctuated between declaring the importance of controls while at the same time expressing a longing to be free of discipline. Release is best seen as a spectrum rather than an absolute, where respondents shift from not caring at one end of the scale to giving into pleasure on occasion at the other end.

Shifting between self-control and a form of controlled release is legitimated by social events. Many mentioned events in their lives where they felt release was sanctioned or well-earned and thus involved little guilt. Examples of these included holidays, when women in particular spoke of enjoying food that they normally denied themselves; 'If I was away too I'd say to heck with it and don't worry about the fat end of it, I would always have the fry for breakfast'. However this is not a permanent state of release and once the holiday is over it is back to a regime of control.

Respondents also used release as a means of coping with or rewarding themselves for getting through a hard day, either at work, or in the home. Life events such as pregnancy worked as a catalyst for release for some women, while for others it had the opposite effect. In the course of the discussions, respondents also made reference to stages in the life cycle where they believed release was more acceptable (see also Backett and Davision, 1995). Release in young people, even if it occurred on a regular basis was deemed less of a health hazard because it was counter-balanced by high levels of activity, and the reserve of youth. On the other hand there were some older people who felt that old age in itself sanctioned a shift towards release.

The evidence of this study would suggest that health promotion strategies need to pay more attention to lived experience rather than emphasising ideals. The health promotion agenda is permeated with 'should language' or the language of control. Rather than encouraging people to adopt more constraint, this language can have the opposite effect, that of release.

> Most people are doing it [giving way to release] saying no I don't believe that. No I don't believe the so-called experts, it is a kind of rebellious thing, I suppose it is more it is put up to people it is bad for you and well for young people it makes it more attractive [referring in particular to smoking].

The Role of External Factors: Lay Understandings of Cancer

Although there was acceptance of the role played by the self in relation to health there was also talk about external factors. Respondents saw the environment as the most important external factor affecting their health and brought up a range of environmental issues in the focus group discussions. The exception here was in the traveller men's group where there was emphasis on the role of the self. This is of interest given that this group has the worst morbidity and mortality rates of any group in Irish society. This poor health status is largely attributed to external factors, for example poverty, and poor sanitation and living conditions. This echoes Blaxter (1997: 748) who found that external causes of health and illness, such as 'housing, the environment, personal poverty or prosperity' tended not to be mentioned by working class respondents although, objectively speaking, these factors were most significant in relation to their health.

The findings of this study indicate that respondents linked cancers in particular to the environment, while heart disease was deemed a lifestyle issue. Popular wisdom linked the high rate of cancer in Louth to the proximity of Louth to

Sellafield; 'Co Louth has the highest population [with cancer] because of Sellafield', 'Louth is pretty, pretty awful' (see also Balshem, 1991).

A fear of Sellafield was evident, and a number of respondents believed that cancer, and specifically cancer in young people was caused by Sellafield. One young respondent stated:

> It [Sellafield] has to be doing something because so many young people are dying around the place, so there has to be something somewhere, so that has to be one of the problems.

There was a desire for an explanation for cancer, and a feeling that cancer in the young particularly needs to be explained. The evidence of this study would suggest that Sellafield is blamed for unexplained instances of illness in Co. Louth.

In general, respondents did not feel in control of the environment. It was seen as something outside of their control. This was particularly true of Sellafield. As one respondent put it 'Sellafield is there, but what can you do about it wear a gas mask? you can't really do anything about it'. The role played by individuals in relation to the environment was not acknowledged. There was a feeling that 'you can do nothing about that [the environment] really'. This is in keeping with the findings of a recent survey on environmental attitudes in Ireland, where only 23 per cent of working class respondents believed that individuals had responsibility for the environment (Department of the Environment and Local Government, 2000: 10). This is despite the fact that while health risks in the nineteenth century were associated with the natural environment, current environmental risks can be described as man made. Nettleton and Bunton (1995) argue that health promotion ignores the importance of the environment for health. The evidence of this study would suggest that the environment is an important issue in relation to lay health beliefs in Co. Louth and that health promotion initiatives in the region should pay attention to this.

There was no evidence of respondents changing their own behaviours because of these environmental problems or risks (see also Department of the Environment and Local Government, 2000: 6). In relation to health, this means that there is no evidence to suggest that environmental awareness led to risk avoidance. Instead, there was a link between environmental awareness and feelings of uncertainty in relation to respondents' own health.

> I just imagine we could be living, you know, a healthy enough life and if it's, I suppose, the atmosphere or Sellafield or something else could get to you, you know [(yeah)]. You're trying to live healthy and as I said you know something else could get you, you know.

However this is not to suggest that respondents were fatalistic as a result. Rather, Sellafield was seen as one of a number of factors contributing to ill health in the area; specifically, ill health in others.

The findings of this study indicate that respondents linked cancers in particular to the environment, while heart disease was related to lifestyle factors. The evidence of this study illustrates that the lay understanding of cancer led to a fear of cancer, in view of this it might be suggested that cancer education initiatives be considered in the Louth area that would address these fears directly.

Lay Understandings of Risk

According to epidemiologists, health can be promoted and disease prevented if we can identify and control risk factors. Here, the concept of risk is underpinned by the notion of probability. However, others have contested the accuracy of this tool in evaluating risk, primarily because it fails to take into account the notion that risk is a cultural phenomenon, intricately bound up in subjective value systems (Heyman, 1998). In other words lay people have their own rationality on what constitutes health risks for them, and although these may be at odds with scientific wisdom, they are rational and appropriate in the socio-cultural context in which they occur. Lay formulation of risk emerged as an important concept in understanding of lay health beliefs.

The case of smoking

Respondents made the distinction between controllable and uncontrollable risks. Controllable risks refer to lifestyle risks you take yourself, for example smoking. Respondents tended to use their own lay logic to legitimate such risky behaviour.

> I was very much involved in Scuba diving for 25 years and I smoked all the way through. I was still probably one of the better ones in the club and could hold my breath for longer than most. I smoked all the way through that … I reckon the fact that I was active kept any risk very much down.

Examples of this often occurred with smokers who viewed activity as an antidote to smoking, rather than something that was negatively affected by smoking. This rationale is the reverse of expert logic, which often highlights the negative impact smoking has on one's activity levels. For other smokers, living in a rural environment with lower pollution also served (they believed) to reduce the risk of smoking and thus gave them a licence to smoke more; 'If you are smoking say 10 or 20 cigarettes a day and you drive fast and you live in the city or whatever well that is probably worse than smoking in the [country]'. For some women, the risk of excessive weight gain associated with giving up cigarettes was greater than the risk associated with smoking itself, thus smoking was deemed less 'risky'.

Rationalising feelings of well being was another strategy participants adopted to legitimate their return to smoking after a period of abstinence. Here, smokers suggested they felt no better after giving up the cigarettes, in fact some complained that their health deteriorated as a result of the abstinence; 'I smoke too, I was in hospital for three weeks, that was my lungs clearing out, I went straight back on them and now I am as fit as a fiddle since I went back on them'.

The mythical smoker

Respondents also refuted expert calculation of 'risks' associated with certain health behaviours simply because they did not fit in with their own lay observations that 'fat smokers really do live till advanced old age and svelte joggers really do fall down' (Davidson et al, 1992: 683). In several of the focus groups respondents spoke of someone they knew who smoked 'like a trooper' but lived 'till ripe old age'. Smokers used this 'mythical smoker' in order to justify their continued smoking.

> I was reared with my granny and grandfather, he lived until he was seventy nine, he drank everyday and he smoked about 40 cigarettes or more everyday.

> Then I look around me and I see people dying anyway that don't smoke. My father never smoked or drank in his life ... and he had the worst death anyone could have of cancer.

Lay formulation of risk is an important concept in our understanding of lay health beliefs. From this study it is apparent that people accept risks either because they enjoy them or because they believe intuitively or calculatively that, on balance, the expected *social* benefits outweigh the possible *medical* costs. Dismissing lay risk assessments as erroneous or unscientific, hinders understanding. In addition, an over concentration on a probability risk model excludes this lay perspective and thus prevents a true understanding of 'risky' behaviour.

Relationship between Lay and Expert Perceptions of Risk

Another related area of interest is the relationship between lay and expert perceptions of risk. Discussions around food in particular highlighted the current tension that exists between lay and expert definitions of risk. Risks mentioned included growth hormones in meat, genetically modified food, antibiotics fed to animals, steroids in food etc. There was a feeling that 'everything' is dangerous and that there are too many risks to be managed in relation to food. Conflicting expert advice serves to undermine lay trust in expert systems, which in turn can result either in consumer apathy or consumer anxiety, both of which can be injurious to health.

> I ignore that kind of thing, there was a bit too much scare mongering, and people got cynical about it. Because every couple of months now the so-called 'experts' are telling you something is bad for you, and what was bad for you a few years ago is now good for you ... you sit back and you say to yourself is there a hidden agenda ... there is a bit too much scare mongering.

In late modernity it is the responsibility of each individual to evaluate risks for him/herself, using information obtained from the mass media, and from family and friends. This reliance on the self in the production of health had led to an increased feeling of the precariousness of health (Beck, 1992). We are seeing perhaps a move away from blind faith in science towards a more questioning and critical attitude among the lay public, where routine scepticism has replaced blind acceptance. This scepticism it must be noted, was not confined to the young or the better educated, but emerged in all groups.

Scepticism about experts allowed respondents to ignore expert advice. This finding has implications for health promotion as a discipline. Health promotion often involves the promotion of expert advice. Given the problems respondents identified in relation to such advice it might be more useful for health promotion initiatives to consider focusing instead at facilitating lay behaviour.

Conclusion

There has been a shift in health promotion recently to recognise socio-structural components of health. This is reflected in the recent call for 'greater... multidisciplinary approaches to address the impact which social, economic and environmental factors have on the physical, mental and social well-being of individuals and communities' (Department of Health and Children, 2000: 21). This chapter can be seen contributing to knowledge in this area. In particular, a focus on lay understandings of health is a welcome corrective to a focus solely on quantitative measures in relation to these socio-structural components.

> If health promotion is to be effective then it needs to be sensitive to the ways in which structure (and behaviour) are experienced in the everyday lifeworlds of individuals; the everyday cultural and social locations of health. (Watson *et al.*, 1996: 163)

The evidence of this study would suggest that lay definitions of health are complex and multidimensional. Health was understood in its social context and a holistic understanding of health was evident in respondents' talk. A qualitative approach was found to capture the complexity of lay health beliefs in a way that a quantitative approach cannot.

There was no unitary understanding of health evident. Instead, health was found to mean different things to different people, and also to mean different things at different times over the lifecycle. Health was understood to be a relative concept. Age differences were central here and definitions of health were found to change over the life-course. A difference can be identified between older and younger groups in relation to lay definitions. Older groups seemed to want to claim good health even in the face of illnesses, while younger people seemed reluctant to claim health despite the absence of illness. It was also found that moral judgements seem to overlay the attainment of health. The evidence of this study would suggest that health promotion strategies need to pay more attention to lived experience rather than emphasising ideals. An emphasis on ideals may have unintended negative consequences and may in fact contribute to inertia.

While there is still some evidence of the hegemony of biomedicine, particularly among older people, there is a growing questioning of its efficacy in the treatment of illness and in the production of health. The findings would suggest a shift away from the biomedical paradigm and a move towards the more holistic paradigm, which stresses the role of the 'self' and lifestyle in the production and maintenance of one's health. There was evidence of a questioning of expertise in general and biomedicine in particular.

Notions of control, release and balance emerged as central components in the discourse surrounding health behaviours. Respondents found themselves astride two opposing mandates, one calling for self-control and the other for release. Health behaviours for the most part were bound up in striving for moderation or balance rather than actually achieving it.

Self-control does not occur in a vacuum but was often found to be the result of external triggers. Negative changes or a crisis in a person's life can open up possibilities for positive health-related changes. There is a tradition in health education of focusing directly on changing health habits but, as the study suggests, changes in health habits maybe a consequence of changes in a person's life which are social rather than health specific. Health educators in the future might be better advised to put some energy into detecting and harnessing life changes, which act as 'cues' to action rather than just focusing on measuring health outcomes.

Health was understood as involving an interplay between external forces and the self. The self has the ability to control some risks, but other risks are determined by forces external to the self. There was no group where the emphasis leaned exclusively in one direction or the other. Following Tucker (1997), this can be termed a holistic rather than reductionist understanding of health. In relation to Sellafield, it was evident that this was a concern of the local community in Dundalk and the Cooley peninsula in particular. Popular wisdom linked the high rate of cancer in Louth to the proximity of Sellafield. However, there was no evidence of fatalism in this respect. Sellafield was seen as one of a number of factors contributing to ill-health in the area and respondents also pointed to the role of the self in the production of both health and ill-health. The evidence of this study illustrates that the lay understanding of cancer led to a fear of cancer. It might be suggested that cancer education initiatives be considered in the Louth area that would address these fears directly.

Lay formulations of risk also emerged as an important concept. Risk is understood not in terms of probability but as a subjective concept rooted in respondents' own experiences. From this study it is apparent that people accept risks either because they enjoy them, or because they believe intuitively or calculatively that, on balance, the expected benefits outweigh the possible costs. Lay people, in other words, have their own rationality on what constitutes health risks for them, which although it may be at odds with 'expert' advice, it is rational and appropriate in the socio-cultural context in which it occurs. An over-concentration on a probability model of risk does not allow for the inclusion of this lay perspective.

Note

[1] A total of five census-based indicators, widely believed to be a determinant of material disadvantage, form the SARU deprivation index. These include (1) Unemployment, (2). Low social class. (3) No car, (4) Rented Accommodation (5) Overcrowding. Using mathematical models, a deprivation score was calculated for each of the district electoral divisions (DEDs). A DED with a score of 1 is least deprived, whilst a score of 5 is most deprived. DEDs with a score of 4 or 5 are classified as deprived.

References

Backett, K. and Davison, C. (1995), 'Lifecourse and Lifestyle: The Social and Cultural Location of Health Behaviours', *Social Science and Medicine*, 40(5): 629-38.

Backett, K. (1992), 'Taboos and Excesses: Lay Health Moralities in Middle Class Families', *Sociology of Health and Illness*, 14(2): 255-74.

Balshem, M. (1991), 'Cancer, Control and Causality: Talking About Cancer in a Working-Class Community', *American Ethnologist*, 18: 152-72.

Beck, U. (1992), *Risk Society: Towards a new Modernity*, London: Sage.

Blaxter, M. (1997), 'Whose Fault Is It? People's Own Conceptions of the Reasons For Health Inequalities', *Social Science and Medicine*, 44(6):747-56.

Bordo, S. (1993), *Unbearable Weight: Feminism, Western Culture and the Body*, Berkeley: University of California Press.

Bunton, R., Nettleton, S. and Burrows, R. (eds) (1995), *The Sociology of Health Promotion: Critical Analyses of Consumption, Lifestyle and Risk*, London: Routledge.

Catterall, M. and MacLaran, P. (1997), Focus Group Data and Qualitative Analysis Programs: Coding the Moving Picture as Well as the Snapshots, *Sociological Research Online*, vol. 2, no. 1, http://www.socresonline.org.uk/socresonline/2/1/6.html.

Cleary, A. and Tracey, M.P. (eds) (1997), *The Sociology of Health and Illness in Ireland*, Dublin: UCD Press.

Crawford, R. (1984) 'A cultural account of health-control, release and the social body', in J. McKinlay (ed.) *Issues in the Political Economy of Health*, London: Tavistock.

Davison, C.G., Smith, D. and Frankel, S. (1991), 'Lay epidemiology and the prevention Paradox: the implications of coronary candidacy for health education', *Sociology of Health and Illness*, 13 (1): 1-19.

Department of the Environment and Local Government (2000), *Attitudes and Actions: A National Survey on the Environment*, Dublin.

Department of Health and Children (2000), *The National Health Promotion Strategy 2000-2005*, Dublin: Department of Health and Children.

Department of Public Health, North Eastern Health Board (2000), *Health Status Report in the North Eastern Health Board*, Navan, Ireland: NEHB.

Faughnan, P. et al. (1998), *Irish Citizens and the Environment: A Cross-National Study of Environmental Attitudes, Perceptions and Behaviours*, Wexford: Environmental Protection Agency.

Friel, S. and Kelleher, C. (1999), *SLAN - Survey of Lifestyle, Attitudes and Nutrition*, Department of Health Promotion: National University of Ireland, Galway.

Fry, C.L. (2000), 'Culture, Age and Subjective Well-Being: Health, Functionality, and the Infrastructure of Eldercare in Comparative Perspective', *Journal of Family Issues* 21(6): 751-76.

Heyman, B. (1998), *Risk, Health and Health Care: A Qualitative Approach*, Arnold: London.

Keogh, E. (2000) 'Louth has been calling for Sellafield since 1957', *Irish Times*, 2000 March 28.

Krueger, R.A. (1988), *Focus Groups: A Practical Guide for Applied Research*, Newbury Park, Sage Publications.

McCluskey, D. (1997) 'Conceptions of health and illness in Ireland', in Cleary, A. and Tracey, M.P. (eds), p 51-68, *The Sociology of Health and Illness in Ireland*, Dublin: UCD Press.

McCluskey, D. (1989), *Health: People's Beliefs and Practices*.

Meillier, L.K., Lund, A.B. and Kok, G. (1997), 'Cues to Action in the Process of Changing Lifestyle', *Patient Education and Counseling*, 30: 37-51.

Morgan, D. (1988), *Focus Groups as Qualitative Research*, London: Sage.

Saltonstall, R. (1993), 'Healthy Bodies, Social Bodies: Men's and Women's Concepts and Practices of Health in Everyday Life', *Social Science Medicine*, 36(1) pp. 7-14.

Stewart, D. (1990), *Focus Groups: Theory and Practice*, London: Sage.

Tucker, V. (1997), 'From Biomedicine to Holistic Health: Towards a New Health Model', in Cleary, A. and Tracey, M.P. (eds), pp 30-50, *The Sociology of Health and Illness in Ireland*, Dublin: UCD Press.

Twaddle, A.C. and Hessler, A.M. (1977), *A Sociology of Health*, St Louis: C.V. Mosby.

Watson J., Cunningham-Burley S., Watson N. and Milburn K. (1996), 'Lay theorising about the body and implications for health promotion', *Health Education Research*, 11(1), 161-172.

Chapter 4

Self-Rated Health in Moscow and Helsinki

Hannele Palosuo

Introduction

The Russian health crisis, which was shown as a sudden decline in life expectancy, particularly of Russian men, was perhaps the most astonishing phenomenon in the development of population health in Europe in the 1990s, following the end of the Cold War and the collapse of the Russian economy. Similar tendencies of declining life expectancy were also noted in other former socialist countries of Eastern and Central Eastern Europe (e.g. Cornia and Paniccià, 2000). Yet the Russian population was particularly afflicted by an unprecedented growth of mortality from practically all major causes of death during the first half of the 1990s (e.g. Shkolnikov and Meslé, 1996; Cockerham, 1999; Shkolnikov and Cornia, 2000). At the same time, life expectancy in Western European countries was steadily increasing (e.g. Bobak and Marmot, 1996; Vallin and Meslé, 2002). This health crisis in Russia, which may still not be over (Shkolnikov et al., 2001), has been studied widely in terms of the development in mortality. This has provided the most reliable data for the description of the population's health and which is also useful for international comparisons (e.g. Cornia and Paniccià, 2000; Shkolnikov and Cornia, 2000).

Much less research has been conducted on morbidity, experience of illness, or self-rated health of the Russian population. Cross-cultural comparative studies have been few. There are historical reasons for the scarcity of this research (Dmitrieva 2001), which go beyond what seem to be general and persistent difficulties of comparing morbidity between different cultures (Blaxter, 1989). For many decades, empirical research depicting social problems were not encouraged in the Soviet Union (see for example Jadov, 1998; Batygin, 1998), and population health was one of the sensitive areas, among many others. Unfavourable statistical information and research results could be censored and, for example, detailed mortality statistics were concealed from the early 1970s, when the health trends had started to decline in the Soviet Union, until the latter part of the 1980s (e.g. Anderson and Silver, 1997). There were local studies on health and the evaluation of health since the 1980s, but self-reported health has been surveyed on nationally representative samples only since 1992 (see for example Zhuravleva, 1989; Shilova, 1989; Dmitrieva, 2001; Palosuo, 2000b). Some international epidemiological and intervention surveys such as the WHO MONICA and CINDI projects and the Lipid Research Clinics Program were conducted in some Soviet cities. However, few comparative studies on health and well being can be found in other than a early comparative survey conducted in North- and East-European capitals, which included items on psychological well-being (Haavio-Mannila, 1992). During the latter part of the 1990s, studies on mortality have abounded, but also studies on morbidity and health of the Russian population have also started to appear. This has also been translated for an international audience (McKeehan et al,. 1993; McKeehan, 2000; Rusinova and Brown, 1996; 1997; Shilova, 1998; 1999; Nazarova, 1998; 2000; Zohoori et al., 1999; 2002; Cockerham 1999; 2000; Carlson, 2000a; 2000b), and in a comparative context as well (Carlson, 1998). In Finland, which is the country of comparison in this chapter, surveys on health have been conducted regularly on national samples since the 1960s (see for example Lahelma and Karisto 1993). In view of the dramatic changes in the health of the Russian population, it is of interest and importance to evaluate the extent to which the tools used for assessing health in cross-cultural studies address the same phenomena in Russia compared to Western countries.

Purpose and Material

This chapter is based on a comparative survey on health and health-related lifestyles of adult populations in 1991 in Moscow and Helsinki, the capitals of the neighbouring countries Russia and Finland (Palosuo et al., 1995; 1998; Palosuo, 2000a). The purpose of the chapter is to shed light on the problems of comparative health research by exploring the content and dimensions of a version of the global measure of self-assessed health. It is the simple single question that asks the respondents to rate their overall health, usually by a five-point, but sometimes also four- or three-point, scale from very good health to very poor health. This widely used question has turned out to be a reliable measure of the overall health and also to predict subsequent mortality (Idler, 1992; Idler and Benyamini, 1997; Lundberg and Manderbacka, 1996; Valkonen et al., 1997; Manderbacka, 1998). It has also been found to tolerate some amount of variability in wordings in cross-cultural comparisons, without losing its reliability in ordering the respondents according to their 'subjective' health (Idler and Benyamini 1997). The focus of this paper is on methodological exploration rather than an assessment of the level of self-rated health in the two study populations.

The data for the study were collected by postal surveys from samples aged 18-64 years in Helsinki and Moscow in 1991. The year was the last in the existence of the Soviet Union. Although social and political changes had been accelerating in the years prior to our study in Russia, the year of the study was still relatively 'normal', in comparison to the 'shock therapy' which started the next year by a liberalisation of prices and a massive privatisation of the state property. This was also associated with concomitant growth in the rates of poverty, crime, morbidity and mortality (e.g. UNICEF, 1993; Bobak et al., 1998; Carlson, 2000a; 2000b; Palosuo, 2002). Russia was Finland's biggest trading partner in 1991 and the year after the study faced the deepest recession in a century (Jäntti et al., 2000). However, the turbulence in Moscow, including the short-lived coup d'état in August 1991, had an effect upon the response rate, which remained at 29 per cent, whereas in Helsinki the rate at 71 per cent (N=824) was quite normal for the capital region in Finland. Some additions were made to the Muscovite sample to increase the numbers (the final sample size was 545). The sex, age and marital status distributions of both data sets corresponded fairly well to the respective population distributions and to each other, but the Moscow sample had an overrepresentation of persons with higher education, whereas in Helsinki those with higher education were slightly under expectations. The educational bias has not been corrected for in the analyses and it has to be kept in mind that the Moscow respondents represent the more educated strata. The collection of the data and the data sets have been described in detail elsewhere (Palosuo et al., 1995; 1998; Palosuo, 2000b; 2002).

Comparability in Cross-Cultural Research

The basic methodological question in cross-cultural research is that of comparability. How do we know that our questions measure the same things in different cultural environments? The question is especially pertinent when structured surveys are used, with their often somewhat artificial linguistic expressions that may not be used in everyday language (see Palosuo 2000b). When constructing our research instrument, which was a structured questionnaire with very few open-ended questions, there was a somewhat naive ideal (at least in the mind of the present author) to formulate 'identical' questions and questionnaires in Russian and Finnish. However, during the process of developing the instrument, and especially in later analysis, doubts arose on whether any of the questions of the Russian and Finnish forms were, strictly speaking, 'identical'.

From a more sophisticated viewpoint, it may indeed be too ambitious an ideal for sociological comparative survey even to aspire to identical measurement. A more useful notion for addressing comparability in cross-cultural research seems to be that of equivalence (see Bice and Kalimo, 1971; Nowak, 1977; Abel, 1991), which is the special form of validity in comparative research. Equivalence may be divided into several subtypes. According to Bice and Kalimo (1971), the 'equivalence of meaning' will be satisfied if questions in a comparative study are understood to mean more or less the same things to the respondents. This may be achieved, for instance, by two-way translations by bilingual persons. In our study English was used as an auxiliary language in addition to Russian and Finnish, and careful methodical cross-translations were required. However, we were not quite certain whether this was carried out because of the unpredictable changes in the Soviet Union at the time. Therefore some of our equivalence problems were due to insufficient preparation (Palosuo, 2000b).

'Conceptual equivalence' requires that responses to questions are indicators of the same concept (Bice and Kalimo, 1971). For example, in our survey, one question was meant to assess health risk awareness in relation to smokers' own smoking. For various reasons this ended up in the questionnaire with different response scales but also different conceptual content. The question went 'Do you think that you smoke - with response alternatives in Helsinki: 1) all too much, 2) slightly too much, 3) moderately 4) I'd like to smoke more; and in Moscow: 1) too much, 2) more than I ought to 3) moderately 4) little 5) I could smoke more. The response scales were thus not exactly the same, but the concept of health risk was also mixed with quite another aspect, that of availability of cigarettes, which were occasionally very scarce in the last years of the Soviet rule. According to Bice and Kalimo, only if the measured items are both conceptually and semantically equivalent, they can be considered identical. If the items are conceptually the same but differ semantically, they can be considered equivalent.

Conceptual equivalence is close to what Nowak (1977) has called 'relational equivalence', and some other researchers 'functional equivalence' (e.g. Allardt, 1990). Nowak reserves identity, or 'phenomenological identity', to such concepts or definitions that refer to certain characteristics of persons that are 'unrelational' and can be considered 'phenomenologically' the same. His examples of such characteristics are sex, age and behaving in a certain way. Most sociological concepts, however, have to do with relational properties and denote phenomena that are related to a 'criterion variable' in a specified way.

The phenomena addressed in empirical inquiry may or may not be identical in 'real' life. If they do not appear as phenomenologically the same, the operationalisations of the concepts ought to be different. This means that one should not be too preoccupied with the simple lexical similarity in the operationalisation of the concepts into measurable questions, but rather strive for meaningful similarity. An obvious problem is that one may not know in advance which identical or different phenomena constitute elements of the same relations. Sometimes this can be assessed in the data analysis. Many concepts are, according to Nowak, of a mixed nature and include both non-relational and relational properties.

Nowak (1977) has discerned several aspects of relational equivalence: 1) *cultural equivalence* refers to the perception and evaluation of objects or phenomena similarly; 2) *contextual equivalence* refers to objects belonging to higher level aggregates or systems previously classified as similar; 3) *structural equivalence* refers to objects occupying the same position within certain structural systems; 4) *functional equivalence* refers to the same role that objects play in the functioning of the systems compared; 5) *correlation equivalence* implies similar correlations to a criterion variable; and 6) *genetic equivalence* refers to the phenomena being defined as coming from the similar source.

According to Nowak, these types are not mutually exclusive but several aspects can relate to one concept. His example is the Marxist notion of social class, which by definition stresses the generic equivalence, but may also be seen as involving structural, contextual and functional and even cultural aspects of equivalence. Obviously, other social class and status concepts may similarly be analysed along these dimensions.

Nowak was concerned with verificational cross-national surveys, which aim at the development of empirically based social theory. This was not the aim of the present study. Nevertheless, the dimensions of equivalence seem to be heuristically applicable, even if strict criteria for an assessment of equivalence may not be available. For instance, the previous example on the assessment of smoking was wanting in contextual equivalence. This is because the interpretation was different due to the effect of different social system elements to smoking (smoking 'too much' was not just a 'free choice' of taking a health risk, but depended on external factors in the other study site).

Bice and Kalimo (1971) divided the levels for assessing the adequacy of the indicators into technical, semantic and conceptual levels, of which the technical level is the least problematic. Many of the problems in the construction of our joint instrument were rather simple and technical. However, even technical departures from an attempted identity in questions often turn out to have their theoretical aspects. One could claim that, practically, in all questions in a survey on social phenomena, including health, theoretical elements are implied. These are obvious in all questions on the socio-economic background of the respondents, which are routinely asked in any survey. This is especially so if the societies have different systems of social and economic organisation, as was the case in comparing the citizens of the (then) socialist Russia to those of Finland which represented a mixed market economy. Examples of the equivalence problems concerning indicators of the social position and health-related lifestyles of the survey have been given elsewhere (Palosuo, 2000a; 2000b).

How Good is 'Normal' Health?

It has been noted that the widely used simple self-assessment of health captures something more and something less than the medical health assessment (see Manderbacka, 1995; Idler and Benyamini, 1997). Despite the high correlation of self-rated health with medically established morbidity, people with medical diagnoses may sometimes evaluate their health quite positively, and vice versa. Self-rated health seems to be an overall assessment, in which medically established morbidity, subjective experience of illness and its functional consequences, as well as somatic and psychological symptoms which exceed some perceived average are taken into account (Manderbacka 1995; 1998). In addition, other aspects, such as health behaviour, may be involved (e.g. Krause and Jay, 1994). People tend to use health behaviour, may be involved (e.g. Krause and Jay, 1994). People tend to use some general points of reference when assessing their health, such as their own previous health or the health of their peers, as Manderbacka (1998) has found in her studies on elderly Swedish and middle-aged Finnish people. Thus, by advancing age and experience of illness, the criteria for the assessment of health may change (e.g. Blaxter, 1990).

In a specifically designed methodological study of the meanings people have in mind when they reply to this single question on overall health (in a semi-structured interview), Finnish adults have been found to employ five domains of evaluation (Manderbacka, 1988). The most important domain was presence or absence of illness, used by all; the others were health as a reserve (including resistance to illness), health as function (functional capability), health as experience (bodily or mental experience) and health as action (fitness and health behaviour). They were similar to the dimensions extracted from the descriptions of health given in the British Health and Lifestyle Survey (Blaxter, 1990). Conceptualisations of health may also vary by the socio-economic status of the respondent. In a study based on a small sub-sample (N=44) of a larger survey conducted in St. Petersburg, Russia, in 1992, Rusinova and Brown (1997) found that those with higher status used more many-sided and psychological notions of their own health. In comparison, those in lower positions used more physical and functional notions of their health. Somewhat similar differences in health concepts in different social groups have been found elsewhere (Blaxter, 1990).

In Western surveys on adult populations, including Finnish surveys, the distributions of self-rated health have tended to lean heavily on having at least (rather) good health (e.g. Tessler and Mechanic, 1978; Blaxter, 1990; Lundberg and Manderbacka, 1996; Arinen et al., 1998; Manderbacka et al., 1998; Aromaa and Koskinen, 2002), whereas in several surveys on Russia the middle category either out of five or three options, or sometimes the second lowest out of four options, termed as 'normal', 'satisfactory', 'medium' or 'average', has been chosen much more often (Zhuravleva and Kogan, 1993; Travin, 1993; McKeehan et al., 1993; Zhuravleva, 1998b, Bobak et al., 1998; Nazarova, 1998, 2000; Fedorova and Fomin, 2000; Rose, 2000; Carlson, 2000a, 2000b; Laaksonen et al., 2001). Health has also been rated as poor more often in Russia, which probably reflects actual differences in health, not just response tendencies, and is in compliance with what is known of the high level of mortality in Russia. In Finland, the proportions reporting poor or rather poor health have been higher than in other Scandinavian countries (Aromaa et al., 1999).

In the present survey, the middle category out of five options was termed 'normal' in the Russian self-assessment of health, and 'average' in the Finnish questionnaire. This middle category was chosen by 68 per cent of men and 60 per cent of women in Moscow, and by 32 per cent of men and 33 per cent of women in Helsinki. Only 7 per cent of Muscovite women and 14 per cent of Muscovite men considered their health good, whereas in Helsinki the numbers were 62 per cent and 59 per cent respectively. In Helsinki 7 per cent rated their health as poor, while these shares in Moscow were 34 per cent in women and 17 per cent in men.

As this was one of the important outcome measures of the survey, and some variation was lost because of the heavy concentration onto one category, it was important to explore the 'meaning' and limits of this assessment. Although the mid-point categories with other linguistic terms in Russian global self-assessments of health have also tended to elicit more responses than is usual in Western surveys, the term 'normal' may have some additional attraction due to its use as a colloquial attribute in Russia.

'Normality' is a complex concept particularly in relation to health. From a statistical point of view, it may be claimed that it is normal to be ill (Zola, 1966). To put it the other way round, to have no symptoms or complaints is highly extraordinary (Blaxter, 1990). There may be moral overtones to health, and health may be felt as duty (Blaxter, 1990), which is also connected with the ability and moral imperative to work (Manderbacka, 1998). In somewhat similar philosophical terms, health can be considered the norm or normative good, the standard of how it should be (von Wright, 1963). A normal state is equilibrium when bodily organs function in a satisfactory way. A normal state is not problematic and does not even warrant causal explanations (von Wright, 1963).

In Russia, 'normal' is a widely used expression in everyday life and the standard answer for the ordinary questions asking 'How are you' or 'How are things?' The answer ('normal') may mean that everything is fine, or that there is nothing special, perhaps implying that things are as good or bad as always. 'Normal' may, in Russian (as probably in Finnish as well), entice not only temporal comparisons within one's frame of life (things are as usual), but also with the social surroundings, literally norms ('normal' health = like everybody else's health, cf. the points of reference in Manderbacka). 'Normal' may even have the meaning of 'western' in Russia (Alapuro, 1993; Watson, 1995). To live normally has connotations of living like people are perceived to live in western countries. The Finnish term 'average' used in the health scale does not convey a similar array of connotations. Thus, it is possible that the middle category was differently perceived in Moscow and Helsinki and the scale (and concept) was not culturally equivalent. However, the alternatives 'very good', 'good', 'rather poor' and 'very poor' surrounded the middle category, and there is no reason to suspect that the rank order would not be the same for both populations (on the continuity of this measure, see Manderbacka et al., 1998). In this sense, this indicator of health would still have functional equivalence.

In Moscow, men rated their health as 'normal' almost as often regardless of age, whereas among women 'normal' health gave way to 'poor' health steeply with advancing age. In Helsinki 'average' health became more common with advancing age, while 'good' health declined (Table 1).

An attempt to clarify the meaning, or at least limits, of 'normal' and 'average' was made by checking self-rated health against other health variables. Because of low numbers in the 'good' end in Moscow and 'poor' end in Helsinki, the variable was condensed into three categories instead of five. The Muscovites reported feeling worried about their health 'lately' more often (68 per cent of women and 49 per cent of men) than the Finns (40 per cent of women and 29 per cent of men). When cross-tabulating health worries by self-rated health, there was no difference between the cities: those with good, normal/average or poor health reported health worries in equal proportions in both cities (Table 1). Calculating the other way round, those without health worries typically considered their health normal in Moscow (75 per cent of men and 83 per cent of women), while corresponding groups in Helsinki would assess their health as good (73 per cent of men and 75 per cent of women). Women who reported health worries chose 'normal' health as often in Moscow (48 per cent) as women in Helsinki chose 'average (47 per cent), but worrying Muscovite men considered being in normal health somewhat more often (61 per cent) than Finnish men in average health (51 per cent).

Another general evaluation of health was made within a question concerning satisfaction with different areas of life. The Muscovites were much less satisfied with their health, 55 per cent of women and 38 per cent of men expressing dissatisfaction, compared to 16 per cent of women and 13 per cent of men in Helsinki. Those with good or poor health in both cities were as often dissatisfied with their health, while those with normal health in Moscow expressed much more often dissatisfaction than the corresponding middle category in Helsinki (Table 1). Thus, the Russian 'normal' was a less satisfactory condition with apparently more feelings of ill health and discomfort than was the Finnish 'average' health.

A checklist of common chronic diseases established chronic illnesses that had been verified or treated by a doctor during the past year. The list comprised hypertension, myocardial infarct, coronary disease or heart failure, malignant tumour, rheumatic arthritis, back problem, emphysema or bronchitis, chronic pyelonephritis or infection of the urinary tract, eczema, allergy or asthma, intestinal troubles (only in Moscow), angina (only in Moscow) and 'other illness' (Palosuo et al., 1995: Table 14). In Moscow, the most common illness was hypertension/hypotension among women and intestinal problems among men; in Helsinki, back illness among men and allergic problems (including asthma) among women. A simple sum variable was formed, excluding 'angina', which is an acute infectious disease. The Muscovite women had the highest average of the sum, 1.30, followed by Helsinki women 0.90, men in Helsinki (0.85) and Moscow (0.80) having similar average morbidity.

If the respondents were 'healthy' in the sense of not having reported any long-standing illness, three-quarters in Helsinki rated their health as good (78 per cent of men and 72 per cent of women), while in Moscow as many respondents rated their health as normal (73 per cent of men and women). This is similar to the distribution by health worry described earlier. However, of those Muscovite men who reported at least one illness, 63 per cent still defined their health as normal, while among women this fell to 51 per cent. In Helsinki those with at least one illness also most often rated their health as 'average' (43 per cent of men and 39 per cent of women). There was a gradient by increasing number of illnesses so that, in Moscow, the normal category gave way to poor health, while in Helsinki the share of good health dramatically dropped and was mainly replaced by average health (Table 2). Thus, having no medically treated or diagnosed long-standing illness did not mean that self-rated health would be good in Russia as it mostly was in Helsinki. At the same time, the Russian 'normal' health tolerated more illness than the Finnish 'average' health. Having two long-standing illnesses was practically as often rated as normal/average in both cities by both sexes (50-60 per cent), but three or more illnesses resulted in clearly poorer self-assessment of health in Moscow.

Additional information was obtained from the occurrence of 17 psychosomatic symptoms during the previous month. Five symptoms were classified as more 'psychological' (insomnia, depression, nervousness, tiredness, feeling that everything has become too much) and twelve as more 'somatic' (chest pain, joint ache, pain in the neck and shoulders, back pain, headache, eczema, swelling of feet, constipation, stomach trouble, common flu, trembling of hands and sweating without physical exertion). The most common single symptoms were, in Moscow, headache, tiredness and nervousness, in Helsinki tiredness, pain in the neck and shoulders, and headache (Palosuo et al., 1995: Table 16). Without going too deeply into the complexity of interpreting symptoms (see for example Honkasalo, 1988; 1991) it may be noted that part of the symptoms may reflect relatively short-term stress connected with sudden life changes and strain in work and family life. Others may carry information about a more enduring strain (see Manderbacka, 1995) and also illness.

The prevalence of psychological symptoms was very similar in both cities when looking at different categories of self-rated health. Those with normal or average self-rated health were as often 'free' of psychological symptoms: 20 per cent among men in both cities and 12 per cent of Muscovite and 14 per cent of Helsinki women, whereas almost all those with poor health had reported at least one psychological symptom (Table 2). Similarly, one fifth of both Muscovite and Helsinki women with good health had reported no psychological symptoms, whereas among Muscovite men the share was higher (46 per cent) than among Helsinki men (32 per cent). As almost all had experienced at least one somatic symptom, those with at least two symptoms are considered here. The occurrence of at least two somatic symptoms was on a high level in all groups with normal/average health (Table 2). With poor health, two or more symptoms were even slightly more common, but even good health was not contradictory to experiencing somatic symptoms particularly in Helsinki (74 per cent of men in Helsinki compared with 54 per cent in Moscow and 90 per cent of women in Helsinki compared with 68 per cent in Moscow). In addition, this measure supports the similarity of the self-rated health in the two populations, except for 'good' health: in Helsinki the large majority with good health had more somatic symptoms than the tiny minority with good health in Moscow.

There was more diversity in reporting single symptoms and their connections with self-rated health between the cities and between men and women. For instance, commonly reported headache was not associated with self-rated health among women in either city, whereas among men in both cities it was clearly more common among those with poor health. Sleeplessness was not common among those Muscovites who rated their health as good (11 per cent), whereas in Helsinki 24 per cent of men and 37 per cent of women with good health had suffered from sleeplessness, but 64-65 per cent of those with poor health (compared with 33 per cent among Muscovite men and 43 per cent among Muscovite women). Similarly, depression was rare among Muscovites with good health (9 per cent among men and one person = 5 per cent among women), whereas depression was relatively common in Helsinki even among those with good health (22 per cent of men and 40 per cent of women). Among those with poor health, the occurrence of depression was as high as 68 per cent among men and 71 per cent among women in Helsinki (compared with 29 per cent and 34 per cent in Moscow respectively). Neck pain was very frequently present in Helsinki, not only with poor self-rated health, but with average health. Chest pain was reported by the Muscovites much more often (25 per cent of those with good health and 64-65 per cent of those with poor health, compared to 7-11 per cent and 48-53 per cent in Helsinki respectively). Most symptoms had a linear gradient in the categories from good to poor health, with exceptions such as common flu, eczemas (except among Finnish men), neck pain and constipation among Finnish women and nervousness among Muscovite women. On the basis of symptoms, the best health was in Helsinki and was connected with the absence of back problems (72 per cent of men with no back problems rated their health as good) and joint ache (71 per cent of women rated their health as good). In Moscow, the best health was found in the absence of nervousness (26 per cent of men) and absence of exhaustion (12 per cent of women). The largest shares with poor health were in Helsinki found among those suffering from clearly somatic symptoms such as swelling of feet among men (21 per cent) and chest pain among women (19 per cent), and in Moscow swelling of feet (50 per cent of men, 58 per cent of women).

However, it cannot be stated with certainty to what extent the differences in the reporting of symptoms were due to 'cultural choices' or were connected primarily with work and living conditions and/or were symptomatic of clinical pathology. For instance, the higher reporting of neck and shoulder pain in Helsinki might be connected with more static strain from a more computerised working life. A higher reporting of chest pain in Moscow may well be connected with higher rates of cardiovascular morbidity, but it might also be a culturally available expression of discomfort. Altogether, in both cities somatic symptoms (simple sum variable) had a somewhat higher correlation with self-rated health than psychological symptoms (as a sum variable), except among Muscovite men (Table 3). Health worry, morbidity and fitness (measured as the ability to walk 500m, run 100m or run 500m) had quite similar correlation's with self-rated health among men and women in both cities (Table 3).

To conclude, it is obvious that the large Russian category of 'normal' health partly covered areas that, in the Finnish scale, were subsumed under either 'good' or 'poor' health. The numbers were too small to study the gradations between very good and rather good or respective poor health, but with the robust categories the associations with other health variables were almost always linear. 'Normal', or in some studies 'satisfactory', seems to be the normative category in the self-assessment of health for the Russians in the same manner as good is the normative category for Finns (see also for example Manderbacka et al., 1998). In another comparative study the normative assessment of health was poor among Lithuanian 45-60-year-old men, while it was good among Dutch men of the same age (Appels et al., 1996). The power of linguistic cultural conventions has been demonstrated in a study, in which it appeared that Mexican-American and Puerto-Rican respondents who chose to use Spanish in a large health survey in the United States, used 'fair' health as their normative category. In contrast to those Hispanics who in the same study chose to answer in English and whose normative category of health was 'good', when clinical pathology of both groups was taken into account (Angel and Guarnaccia, 1989).

However, it would be erroneous to conclude that the different distributions of self-rated health in our comparison would be only due to culturally variable habits of speech and 'only normative', in spite of the problems in cultural equivalence of the scales. The Russian 'normal' is not equivalent with the Finnish 'good', nor even fully equivalent with the Finnish 'average' health, but overlaps them both. The heavy concentration on the middle category in Moscow, which left more space to poor health compared with the distribution in Helsinki, but very little to good health, is most likely to be indicative of the Russian health problems known from mortality studies and health statistics.

Discussion

The aim of this chapter was to explore the comparability of the single-item self-assessment of health on the basis of a survey on adult populations aged 18-64 years, conducted in 1991 in Helsinki and Moscow. The main focus was in exploring the 'content' or limits of 'normal' health that had attracted 'too many' responses in the Russian response scale. The same tendency to choose the middle category can be observed in the self-assessments of health in other Russian surveys as well, even when terms other than 'normal', such as 'average' ('srednee') or 'satisfactory' have been used. The need for methodological exploration is evident, especially as specific methodological analyses of cross-cultural health surveys including Russia have been rare, which is perhaps understandable in view of the scarcity of comparative research thus far. A number of reports on some other East European and especially Western countries have also discussed methodological questions on various aspects of comparing health and well-being (e.g. Bice and Kalimo, 1971; Abel, 1991; Allardt, 1976; Blaxter, 1989; Lahelma et al., 1993; Kunst, 1997). The role of culture in definitions of illness and health has also been addressed in comparative anthropological and ethnographic studies (see for example Angel and Thoits, 1987).

The idea, and ideal, of aiming at identical questions and questionnaires turned out to be somewhat unrealistic by a closer look to the problems of comparability. Indeed, it seems to be more important to strive for meaningful equivalent indicators, if strictly identical measures with semantically the same expressions are impossible to achieve. It is, however, not only about semantic expressions, but a whole range of cultural, structural, contextual and functional aspects of equivalence, as presented by Nowak (1977) and in slightly different terms by others, needs to be considered in developing research instruments and interpreting cross-cultural data. Most of our questions appeared to be of mixed character, and even seemingly identical questions raised questions of equivalence because of the profoundly different social environments in the two study sites. The particular time of the study, with the rapid transformation of the Russian society, posed an extra frame to our comparison and raised some additional questions of equivalence even in unexpected areas (see Palosuo, 2000b).

There were limitations in this exploration that need to be commented upon. No attention has been paid to the socio-economic variation in the distributions of the health indicators, which appeared with some variability also in this data (Palosuo et al., 1998). It is possible that good, normal/average and poor health do not mean the same things when respondents in different socio-economic groups choose them. This is suggested by the socially variable differences in health concepts found in St. Petersburg by Rusinova and Brown (1997) or in other studies elsewhere (Blaxter, 1990; Krause and Jay, 1994; Manderbacka, 1998). However, another kind of methodology would be needed to assess this. The Moscow sample was biased by education and probably represented the healthier Muscovites. In addition, health and concepts of health vary by age, which was not addressed in this exploration. Age cannot be explained away as a 'confounding' factor but needs to be taken into account by looking at different age groups separately. There were indications of a faster 'ageing' process in Moscow through a more rapid growth of poor self-rated health, compared to Helsinki (Palosuo et al., 1998).

With these reservations in mind, the main conclusion from the exploration is that the large 'normal' category in Moscow carries quite similar connotations with regard to the presence of health worries and reporting psychological and somatic symptoms, when men and women are compared separately in the two cities. Even poor self-rated health is quite similarly connected with these other indicators, whereas the small group of respondents with good health in Moscow seemed to be somewhat better off in terms of experiencing symptoms and illness than the large group of Finns reporting good health. This might be connected with differences in the structure of morbidity, such as the high prevalence of allergies among the Helsinki citizens compared with the high prevalence of other ailments among the Muscovites, or with other qualitative differences in the prevalence and severity of illness. However, there was more dissatisfaction with health among those with 'normal' self-rated health in Moscow, compared with 'average' health in Helsinki, which pointed to more discomfort connected with this large category. Yet, the overall consistency seems to lend support for the functional equivalence of the measure in spite of the cultural variation in terminology. From a technical point of view, it is desirable that a scale differentiates well, which is not achieved with a high concentration onto one category. This limits, for instance, using categorical multivariate analysis, such as logistic regression analysis, in which the cutting point becomes problematic. In Western studies, the division is often set between 'good' and 'less than good' health, as the distributions are usually skewed towards the healthy end. With Russian data, the cut-off point might be better between 'poor' and 'not-poor' health, if the middle category also encompasses elements of good health. Obviously, special attention ought to be paid to the exact wordings of this global scale in cross-cultural settings to avoid too protuberant distributions.

It has been questioned whether the linguistic expressions used in self-reports of states of health and illness can be taken as indicators of equivalent realities in cross-cultural comparisons (Angel and Thoits, 1987). In principle, criteria for the equivalence of various physical conditions can be found in physical pathology, but in psychological problems or less severe conditions, such as general distress, depression or other psychological symptoms, there are few if any external criteria to validate the information. The same may apply to the self-assessment of health. There is an ontological uncertainty that perhaps cannot be solved, but this ultimately philosophical limitation has to be tolerated without letting it hinder attempts to assess health in comparable terms. On the other hand, it may be claimed that self-assessed health is true in its own right and cannot be invalidated by external criteria (Idler, 1992), even if self-rated health does not give the whole picture of health (Blaxter, 1989). It is also noteworthy that the subjective rating of health seems to have very 'hard' external criteria in being predictive of mortality (Idler, 1992). There is no doubt, however, that the self-rating of health with one simple question continues to be an important and useful method of assessing overall health.

No definitive answer can be given by these analyses based on responses in structured questionnaires as to the cognitions about normal or average self-rated health, nor good or poor health in the Russian and Finnish cultures. Yet it is reasonable to conclude that 'normal' and 'average' had a similar middle position in the scales in both cities and the scales ordered the respondents quite similarly. The analyses carried out by several other health variables lend support for the functional equivalence of the scales. Obviously one should be careful about using culturally loaded expressions in a scale, but a deeper insight into the cultural, functional and contextual equivalence in this question would require additional qualitative methodological research of the type that Manderbacka (1998) conducted on the global assessment of health in a Finnish health survey on adults, Jylhä (1994) on elderly people or Krause and Jay (1994) on ethnic and educational subgroups. The results of this exploration are in line with the conclusion made by Idler and Benyamini (1997) who considered in their review that the consistency of this global rating of health is all the more surprising considering the cross-cultural differences in the applied linguistic terms.

Table 1 **Percentages of those expressing worries and dissatisfaction about their health,[1] among the groups rating their health as 'good', 'average/normal' and 'poor'** (in parentheses the base numbers of calculations)

	Self-rated health		
	Good (base N)	Average/normal (N)	Poor (base N)
Has health worries	%	%	%
MEN			
Helsinki	13 (221)	42 (116)	76 (25)
Moscow	14 (35)	44 (162)	98 (41)
WOMEN			
Helsinki	25 (271)	57 (150)	91 (30)
Moscow	24 (17)	56 (96)	97 (98)
Dissatisfied with health			
MEN			
Helsinki	4 (218)	17 (112)	80 (25)
Moscow	6 (34)	32 (152)	87 (38)
WOMEN			
Helsinki	3 (271)	23 (150)	88 (33)
Moscow	5 (19)	40 (158)	90 (93)

[1] Health was one of six areas in a question concerning satisfaction, phrased in Helsinki as 'When you think of the following spheres of life, how satisfied are you with your life? Do your experiences correspond to what you have hoped and expected?' - and in Moscow: 'When you think of your life, how satisfied are you with it? To what extent did your hopes get realised?' Four-point answers were: Corresponds 1) fully 2) rather well 3) rather badly 4) not at all - 3 and 4 combined to mean 'dissatisfied'.

Table 2 **The occurrence (%) of psychological and somatic symptoms during the past month among those with 'good', 'average/normal' and 'poor' self-assessed health** (Occurrence of at least one psychological symptom out of five, and two somatic symptoms out of 12, in parentheses the base numbers of calculations)

	Self-rated health						
	Good (base *N*)		*Average/normal* (base *N*)		*Poor* (base *N*)		*All* (base *N*)
Psychological symptoms past month (>1)	%		%		%		%
MEN							
Helsinki	68	(221)	80	(116)	92	(25)	74 (363)
Moscow	54	(35)	80	(166)	93	(42)	79 (245)
WOMEN							
Helsinki	80	(273)	86	(153)	100	(34)	83 (461)
Moscow	79	(19)	88	(177)	94	(101)	89 (300)
Somatic symptoms past month (>2)							
MEN							
Helsinki	74	(221)	87	(116)	84	(25)	79 (363)
Moscow	54	(35)	83	(166)	93	(42)	81 (245)
WOMEN							
Helsinki	90	(273)	94	(153)	94	(34)	91 (461)
Moscow	68	(19)	87	(177)	94	(101)	88 (300)

Table 3   **Partial correlations of self-rated health (direction: poor) with health worry, morbidity (sum), somatic symptoms (sum), psychological symptoms (sum) and fitness (ability to walk 500m, run 100m or 500m), controlling for age**

	Helsinki men	*Helsinki women*	*Moscow men*	*Moscow women*
Health worry				
(no-yes)	0.40	0.41	0.45	0.44
Morbidity (sum)	0.34	0.34	0.34	0.38
Somatic symptoms				
(sum)	0.44	0.37	0.36	0.37
Psychological				
symptoms (sum)	0.37	0.27	0.38	0.22
Fitness ($\rightarrow$poor)	.42	0.36	0.31	0.31
(*N*)	(358)	(451-456)	(235-240)	(287-294)

Acknowledgement

The other members of the research group are Antti Uutela (National Public Health Institute, Helsinki) and Irina Zhuravleva, Lyudmila Shilova and Nina Lakomova (Institute of Sociology, Russian Academy of Science, Moscow). I wish to express my gratitude to them for comments to an earlier version of this paper.

References

Abel, T. (1991), 'Measuring health lifestyles in a comparative analysis: Theoretical issues and empirical findings', *Social Science and Medicine*, 32: 899-908.

Alapuro, R. (1993), 'Kansalaisyhteiskunnan mahdollisuudet Venäjällä' (Possibilities of a civil society in Russia, in Finnish), In Piirainen T. (ed.) *Itä-Euroopan murros ja Suomi. Gaudeamus: Tampere*, pp 121-141.

Allardt, E. (1976), 'Hyvinvoinnin ulottuvuuksia' (Dimensions of Welfare, in Finnish), WSOY: Porvoo 1976.

Allardt, E. (1990), 'Challenges for comparative social research, *Acta Sociologica*, 33, 3: 183-193.

Anderson, B.A. and Silver, B.D. (1997), 'Issues of data quality in assessing mortality trends and levels in the new independent states', in Bobadilla, J.L., Costello, C.A. and Mitchell, F. (eds) *Premature Death in the New Independent States*, National Academy Press, Washington D.C., pp 120-155.

Angel, R. and Guarnaccia, P.J. (1989), 'Mind, body, and culture: somatization among Hispanics', *Social Science and Medicine*, 28: 1229-1238.

Angel, R. and Thoits, P. (1987), 'The impact of culture on the cognitive structure of illness', *Culture, Medicine and Psychiatry*, 11: 465-494.

Appels, A., Bosma, H., Grabauskas, V., Gostautas, A. and Sturmans, F. (1996), 'Self-rated health and mortality in a Lithuanian and a Dutch population', *Social Science and Medicine* 42: 681-689.

Arinen, S., Häkkinen, U., Klaukka, T., Klavus, J., Lehtonen, R. and Aro, S. (1998), 'Health and the use of health services in Finland. Main findings of the Finnish Health Care Survey 1995/96 and changes from 1987', National Research and Development Centre for Welfare and Health and The Social Insurance Institution, Finland, Official Statistic of Finland Health Care 1998: 5. Helsinki.

Aromaa, A., Koskinen, S. and Huttunen, J. (eds) (1999), *Health in Finland*, National Public Health Institute and Ministry of Social Affairs and Health, Edita Ltd., Helsinki.

Aromaa, A. and Koskinen, S. (ed.) (2002), 'Health and functional capacity in Finland. Baseline results of the Health 2000 health examination survey' (in Finnish, with English Abstract), Publications of the National Public Health Institute B3/2002, Helsinki.

Batygin, G. (1998), 'Preemstvennost' rossijskoj sociologicheskoj tradicii', in Jadov, V.A. (ed.), *Sociologija v Rossii. Izdanie vtoroe, pererabotannoe i dopolnennoe*, Institut sociologii, Rossijskaja Akademija Nauk, Izdatel'stvo Instituta sociologii RAN, Moskva pp 23-44.

Bice, Th. and Kalimo, E. (1971), 'Comparison of health-related attitudes: a cross-national, factor analytic study', *Social Science and Medicine*, 5: 283-318.

Bobak, M. and Marmot, M. (1996), 'East-west divide and potential explanations', in Hertzman, C., Kelly, S. and Bobak, M. (eds), *East-West Life Expectancy Gap in Europe, Environmental and Non-Environmental Determinants*, NATO ASI Series 2: Environment - Vol. 19. Kluwer: Dordrecht, 17-44.

Bobak, M., Pikhart, H. Hertzman, C., Rose, R. and Marmot, M. (1998), 'Socio-economic factors, perceived control and self-reported health in Russia. A cross-sectional survey', *Social Science and Medicine*, 47: 269-279.

Bobak, M., Pikhart, H. Rose, R. Hertzman, C. and Marmot, M. (2000), 'Socio-economic factors, material inequalities and perceived control in self-reported health: cross-sectional data from seven post-communist countries', *Social Science and Medicine*, 51: 1343-1350.

Blaxter, M. (1989), 'A comparison of measures of inequality in morbidity', in Fox, A.J. (ed.), *Health Inequalities in European Countries*, Gower, Aldershot, pp 199-230.

Blaxter, M. (1990), *Health and Lifestyles*, Routledge: London.

Carlson, P. (1998), 'Self-perceived health in East and West Europe: Another European health divide', *Social Science and Medicine*, 46: 1355-1366.

Carlson, P. (2000a), 'An unhealthy decade. A sociological study of the state of public health in Russia in 1990-1999', *Acta Universitatis Stockholmiensis*, 10. Almqvist and Wiksell International: Stockholm.

Carlson, P. (2000b), 'Educational differences in self-rated health during the Russian transition. Evidence from Taganrog 1993-1994', *Social Science and Medicine*, 51: 1363-1374.

Carlson, P. (2001), 'Risk behaviours and self rated health in Russia 1998', *Journal of Epidemiology and Community Health*, 55: 806-817.

Cockerham, W.C. (1999), *Health and Social Change in Russia and Eastern Europe*, Routledge: New York, London.

Cockerham, W. (2000), 'Health lifestyles in Russia', *Social Science and Medicine*, 51: 1313-1324.

Cornia, G.A. and Paniccià, R. (2000), 'The transition mortality crisis: evidence, interpretation and policy responses', in Cornia, G.A. and Paniccià, R. (eds), *The Mortality Crisis in Transitional Economie*, Oxford University Press 3-37.

Dmitrieva, E. (2001), 'The Russian health care experiment: transition of the health csre System and rethinking medical sociology', in Cockerham, W.C. (ed.), *The Blackwell Companion to Medical Sociology*, Blackwell Publishers: Oxford pp 320-333.

Feodorova, N. and Fomin, E. (2000), 'The quality of life and health', *The Finnish Review of East European Studies*, 7: 23-34.

Haavio-Mannila, E. (1992), 'Work, family and well-being in five north- and east-European capitals', *Annales Academiae Scientiarum Fennicae*, Ser. B, Vol. 255, Helsinki.

Honkasalo, M-L. (1988), 'Oireiden ongelma' (The problem of symptoms. A sociomedical study of symptoms, their occurrence and meanings by two research methods), in Finnish, with English Summary, *Kansanterveystieteen laitoksen julkaisuja*, M:101, Helsinki.

Honkasalo, M.-L. (1991), 'Medical symptoms: a challenge for semiotic research', *Semiotica*, 87: 251-268.

Idler, E.L. (1992), 'Self-assessed health and mortality: a review of studies', *International Review of Health Psychology* 1: 33-54.

Idler, E.L. and Benyamini, Y. (1997), 'Self-rated health and mortality: a review of twenty-seven community studies', *Journal of Social and Health Behavior*, 38: 21-37.

Jadov, V.A. (ed.), *Sociologija v Rossii. Izdanie vtoroe, pererabotannoe i dopolnennoe.*, Institut sociologii, Rossijskaja Akademija Nauk. Izdatel'stvo Instituta sociologii RAN, Moskva.

Jylhä, M. (1994), 'Self-rated health revisited: exploring survey interview episodes with elderly respondents', *Social Science and Medicine*, 39: 983-990.

Jäntti, M., Martikainen, P. and Valkonen, T. (2000), 'When the welfare state works: unemployment and mortality in Finland', in Cornia, G.A. and Paniccià, R. (eds), *The Mortality Crisis in Transitional Economies*, Oxford University Press, pp. 351-369.

Kunst, A. (1997), *Cross-national comparisons of socioeconomic differences in mortality*, Thesis Erasmus University Rotterdam.

Krause, N.M. and Jay, G.M. (1994), 'What do global self-rated health items measure?', *Medical Care*, 32(9): 930-942.

Laaksonen, M., McAlister, A., Laatikainen, T., Drygas, W., Morava E., Nüssel, E., Oganov, R., Pardell, H., Uhanov, M. and Puska, P. (2001), 'Do health behaviour and psychosocial risk factors explain the European East-West gap in health status?', *European Journal of Public Health*, 11: 65-73.

Lahelma, E. and Karisto, A. (1993), 'Morbidity and social structure. Recent trends in Finland', *European Journal of Public Health*, 3: 119-123.

Lahelma, E., Manderbacka, K., Rahkonen, O. and Sihvonen, A-P. (1993), 'Ill-Health and its social patterning in Finland, Norway and Sweden', *National Research and Development Centre for Welfare and Health, Research Reports*, 27, Jyväskylä.

Lundberg, O. and Manderbacka, K. (1996), 'Assessing reliability of a measure of self-rated health', *Scandinavian Journal of Social Medicine*, 24: 218-224.

Manderbacka, K. (1995), *Terveydentilan mittarit. Kuinka terveydentilaa on mitattu vuoden 1986 elinolotutkimuksessa?*, Tutkimuksia 213, Tilastokeskus: Helsinki.

Manderbacka, K. (1998), 'Questions on survey questions on health', *Swedish Institute for Social Research*, 30, University of Helsinki and Stockholm University: Stockholm.

Manderbacka, K., Lahelma, E. and Martikainen, P. (1998), 'Examining the continuity of self-rated health', *International Journal of Epidemiology*, 27: 208-213.

McKeehan, I. (2000), 'A multilevel city health profile of Moscow', *Social Science and Medicine*, 51: 1295-1312.

McKeehan, I., Campbell, R. and Tumanov, S.V. (1993), Obraz zhizni, privychki vlijajushchie na zdorov'e moskvichej, i zakon o medicinskom strahovanii 1991-1993 gg. Sociologicheskie issledovanija 3: 45-49.

Nazarova, I.B. (1998), Sub"ektivnye i ob"ektivnye ocenki zdorov'ja naselenija. Sociologicheskij zhurnal 3/4: 246-249.

Nazarova, I. (2000), 'Self-rated health and occupational conditions in Russia', *Social Science and Medicine*, 51: 1375-1385.

Nowak, S. (1977), 'The strategy of cross-national survey research for the development of social theory', in Szalai, A., Petrella, R., Rokkan, S. and Scheuch, E.K. (eds), *Cross-National Comparative Survey Research: Theory and Practice*, Pergamon Press: Oxford pp 3-47.

Palosuo, H., Zhuravleva, I., Uutela, A., Lakomova, N. and Shilova, L. (1995), 'Perceived health, health-related habits and attitudes in Helsinki and Moscow: A comparative study of adult populations in 1991', *Publications of the National Public Health Institute*, A 10/1995. Helsinki. (In Russian 1998, Rossijskaja Akademija Nauk, Institut Sociologii, Moskva).

Palosuo, H., Uutela, A., Zhuravleva, I. and Lakomova, N. (1998), 'Social patterning of ill health in Helsinki and Moscow. Results from a comparative survey in 1991', *Social Science and Medicine*, 45: 1121-1136.

Palosuo, H. (2000a), 'Health-related lifestyles and alienation in Moscow and Helsinki', *Social Science and Medicine*, 51: 1325-1341.

Palosuo, H. (2000b), 'How good is 'normal' health? An exercise in Russian-Finnish comparative survey methodology', *Idäntutkimus - The Finnish Review of East European Studies*, 2001:7: 41-70.

Palosuo, H. (2002), *Health and Well-Being in Moscow and Helsinki*, Manuscript.

Rose, R. (2000), 'How much does social capital add to individual health? A survey study of Russians', *Social Science and Medicine*, 51: 1421-1435.

Rusinova, N. and Brown, J. (1997), Social'no-statusnye gruppy: razlichija v sub"ektivnom zdorov'e, *Peterburgskaja sociologija* 1: 38-59.

Shilova, L.S. (1989), 'Razlichija v samosohranitel'nom povedenii muzhin i zhenshchin', in Borodin, Ju.I. Zdorov'e cheloveka v uslovijah NTR. Akademija Nauk SSSR, Sibirskoe otdelenie, Akademija medicinskih Nauk SSSR, Sibirskoe otdelenie. *Nauka,* Novosibirsk 88-93.

Shilova, L.S. (1998), 'Stress, zdorov'e i transformacija samosohranitel'nogo povedenija naselenija Moskvy za gody reform', in Yanitsky, O.N. (ed.) Rossija: Riski i opasnosti "perehodnogo" obshchestva (*Russia: Risks and Threats of "Transition" Society*, in Russian), Rossijskaja Akademija Nauk, Institut sociologii: Moskva, pp 161-191.

Shilova, L. (1999), 'Problemy transformacii social'noj politiki i individual'nyh orientacij po ohrane zdorov'ja', in Stepanov, E.I. (ed.), Social'nye konflikty: ekspertiza, prognozirovanija, tehnologii razreshenija 15. Konfliktologija zdorov'ja i zdravoohranenija v sovremennoj Rossii. Rossijskaja Akademija Nauk. Institut sociologii, Centr konfliktologii: Moskva 86-114.

Shkolnikov, V.M. and Cornia, G.A. (2000), 'Population crisis and rising mortality in transitional Russia', In Cornia, G.A. and Paniccià, R. (eds), *The Mortality Crisis in Transitional Economies*, Oxford University Press: Great Britain 253-279.

Shkolnikov, V., McKee, M. and Leon, D.A. (2001), 'Changes in life expectancy in Russia in the mid- 1990s', *Lancet*, 357: 917-921.

Shkolnikov, V.M. and Meslé, F. (1996), 'The Russian epidemiological crisis as mirrored by mortality trends', In DaVanzo, J. (ed.), *Russia's Demographic "Crisis"*, Conference Report. Rand Center for Russia and Eurasia http://www.rand.org/publications/CF/CF124/

Tessler, R. and Mechanic, D. (1978), 'Psychological distress and perceived health status', *Journal of Health and Social Behavior*, 19: 254-262.

Travin, I. (1993), 'Tämän päivän venäläinen kaupunki (Russian city today)', in Piirainen, T. (ed.), *Itä-Euroopan murros ja Suomi (Transition in Eastern Europe and Finland*, in Finnish). Gaudeamus, Tampere pp. 213-223.

UNICEF (1993), *United Nations Children's Fund. Central and Eastern Europe in Transition. Public Policy and Social Conditions*, Regional Monitoring Report No. 1. Florence, Italy.

Vallin, J. and Meslé, F. (2002), 'Trends in mortality in Europe since 1950', in Vallin, J., Meslé, F. and Valkonen, T., *Trends in Mortality and Differential Mortality*, Population Studies No. 36, Council of Europe Publishing, Strasbourg pp 31-184.

Valkonen,T., Sihvonen, A.-P. and Lahelma, E. (1997), 'Health expectancy by level of education in Finland', *Social Science and Medicine* 44: 801-808.

Watson, P. (1995), 'Explaining rising mortality among men in Eastern Europe', *Social Science and Medicine*, 41: 923-934.

von Wright, G.H. (1963), *The Varieties of Goodness*, Routledge and Kegan Paul: London.

Zhuravleva, I.V. (1989), Povedencheskij faktor i zdorov'e naselenija. In Borodin Ju.I. *Zdorov'e cheloveka v uslovijah NTR*. Akademija Nauk SSSR, Sibirskoe otdelenie, Akademija medicinskih Nauk SSSR, Sibirskoe otdelenie. Nauka: Novosibirsk, pp 72-77.

Zhuravleva, I. (1993), Otnoshenie k zdorov'ju kak element samosohranitelnogo povedenija. In Zhuravleva I. (ed.) *Otnoshenie naselenija k zdorov'ju*. Rossijskaja Akademija Nauk, Institut sociologii, Moskva. 29-34.

Zhuravleva, I. (1998), 'Otnoshenie k zdorov'ju kak kriterij social'noj stratifikacii', in Golenkova, Z.T. (ed.), *Transformacija social'noj struktury i stratifikacija rossijskogo obshchestva. Vtoroe izdanie, pererabotannoe i dopolnennoe*. Rossijskaja Akademija Nauk, Institut sociologii: Moskva pp 458-479.

Zhuravleva, I.V. and Kogan, V.V. (1993), 'Psihologicheskie faktory zdorov'ja', in Zhuravleva, I. (ed.), *Otnoshenie naselenija k zdorov'ju*, Rossijskaja Akademija Nauk, Institut sociologii: Moskva pp 77-86.

Zohoori, N., Henderson, L., Gleiter, K. and Popkin, B. (1999), *Monitoring Health Conditions in the Russian Federation: The Russia Longitudinal Monitoring Survey 1992-1998*, Report submitted to the U.S Agency for International Development. Carolina Population Center, University of North Carolina at Chapel Hill: North Carolina.

Zohoori, N., Henderson, L., Gleiter, K. and Popkin, B. (2002), *Monitoring Health Conditions in the Russian Federation: The Russia Longitudinal Monitoring Survey 1992-2001*, Report submitted to the U.S Agency for International Development. Carolina Population Center, University of North Carolina at Chapel Hill, North Carolina.

Zola, I.K. (1966), 'Culture and symptoms - an analysis of patients presenting complaints', *American Sociological Review*, 31: 615-630.

Chapter 5

Pragmatism, Globalism and Culturalism: Health Pluralism of Chinese People in Britain

Ruby C.M. Chau and Sam W.K. Yu

Introduction

The aim of this chapter is to study the pattern of medical pluralism of Chinese people in Britain and their methods of securing social inclusion in the health care system. We are also interested in the factors, especially those related to pragmatism, globalism and culturalism, that affect their decisions when choosing their methods for promoting health and seeking social inclusion. The chapter is based on a literature review and the findings of two studies concerning Chinese elderly people in Glasgow and Chinese women in Sheffield. Both studies were part of a larger research project funded by the Joseph Rowntree Foundation from 1997 to 1999.

Accordingly, the chapter is divided into five parts. The first discusses the concepts of medical pluralism in terms of the various types of social relationships involved in health services. The second examines the concepts of social exclusion and social inclusion. The third focuses on Chinese people's strategies of pursuing social inclusion in the health care system. The fourth looks at the cultural, global and pragmatic factors of these strategies. The fourth section reports the key findings of the two studies.

Medical Pluralism

Medical pluralism refers to the fact that different health beliefs and practices can be held simultaneously by different family members or by the same person; people may, in fact, try anything that provides relief from their illness (Streefland, 1985; Parker, 1988; Janes, 1999; Elling, 1981a; Lee, 1981; Phillips and Saul, 1999). For instance, many Chinese people still rely on traditional medicines to strengthen their health and use cultural terms and language to express their mental health; whilst at the same time many of them seek advice from western medical practitioners (Eastwood, 1993; Watt et al., 1993; Congress et al., 1992; Chau et al., 1999; Yu, 2000). Hence pluralistic health care is frequently displayed in the interactions between different systems of medical and health knowledge, which characterize health, illness and the medical institutions (Gallagher and Subedi, 1995). Different interactions may not only represent different attempts to achieve health but also indicate the different types of relationship between participants in the healthcare system.

Relationships between suppliers of medical services

Medical pluralism may be illustrated by the complementary relationship that exists between western and traditional medicines. Studies show that traditional medicines can function in conjunction with modern medicines. Streefland (1985) argues that different medical systems can co-exist very well, as each may have its own niche. Stone (1976) discovered that while there is some competitiveness between medical doctors and local practitioners in Central Nepal, the actual treatment of illnesses reflects a high degree of integration of different medical systems. Parker (1988) suggests that the indigenous referral network used by traditional medicine practitioners could serve as an important referral system for spreading the information concerning the roles and uses of modern allopathic medicine to the needy. In the light of these opinions, it is not surprising to see that the WHO actively explores the feasibility of enabling traditional medicines and modern medicines to reinforce each other (Elling, 1981b).

However, the literature also records competitive, inharmonious and sometimes antagonistic relationships between medical systems. For example, Foster points out:

> The evidence is overwhelming that in countries where traditional peoples have had access to modern medicine for a generation or longer, and where this medicine has been of reasonably good quality, the battle has been won, and scientific medicine is the victor (cited in Parker, 1988, p 919).

While traditional medicines have the opportunity to meet health needs, in spite of the dominance of biomedicine, their essence may largely be distorted by conformity to modern medical systems. As Janes (1999, p 1804) argues:

> Traditional medicines are transformed from culturally-specific methods of identifying, naming and treating illness to repositories of herbal concoctions where assumptions of efficacy rest in scientific understanding of biochemistry rather than in native epistemologies of the body and its relationship to family, kinship group, society and cosmos. In extreme cases, traditional medicine is co-opted by the medical establishment and distributed without concern for (or understanding of) possible iatrogenic consequences.

Worse still, modern medicines are sometimes used as a tool to promote imperialism (Elling, 1981a). An example of this is the introduction of western medicines into China in the 19th Century. Cai (1988, p 524) argued that it was mixed with political motives by citing some views of missionary physicians:

> The best way of introducing Christianity to China is through medicine, while the best way of selling more merchandise in China is through missionary activity. Medicine is the pioneer of Christianity, while Christianity is the pioneer for the promotion of sales.

Relationships between suppliers and users of medical services

Studies have discovered that the relationship between providers of medical services and their users is shaped significantly by how medical services are organised. Western medicines are usually based on a bureaucratically ordered set of schools, hospitals, clinics and professional associations with the emphasis on procedural justice and standardisation (Leslie, 1980). These characteristics favour the development of standardised and rational relationships between practitioners and users of the services.

On the other hand, the traditional forms of health care are often marked by less 'social distance' between users and suppliers (Kroeger and Franken, 1981). This not only implies the high social accessibility of many traditional health services but also the preference of traditional medicine practitioners for using a holistic approach to meet health needs. Streefland's 1985 study shows that traditional practitioners may belong to the same village and actually be kinsmen, neighbours or fellow-cultivators of the users. Moreover, some users choose to rely on traditional medicines because of their belief in the superiority of their culture and their wish to attach their life to traditions (Elling, 1981b). Hence, they see using medical services as more than meeting their health needs; it is also an attempt to share their cultural attachment to traditions with service providers. Thorne and Montague (in Leslie, 1980) show that traditional midwives in Islamic communities carry out a number of tasks rather than play one specific role; these tasks include doing household chores for the mother in the period following the birth, giving advice on health matters, preparing corpses for funerals and serving in the traditional rites of women. In view of the roles they play, we can say that the traditional midwives are prepared to establish different types of relationships with their users in the process of providing health care.

Relationships between users

Users may also develop different relationships between themselves in response to different medical systems. It is not uncommon for patients in capitalist societies to organise themselves into pressure groups to enhance their medical rights and to exert influence on the formulation and implementation of medical policies. Their emphasis on rational relationships and social rights can, to a certain extent, be seen as a response to the professionalisation of western medicines, which as stated above emphasises procedural justice and standardisation. In fact, the medical systems such as the complaint channels are more responsive to organised opinions than individual grievances.

Suppliers of traditional medicines developed within the same culture may share the same language and concepts with users. As a result, users find it easier to communicate with each other and relate their illness and sickness to their everyday experience (Yu, 2000). Sometimes users may also be the suppliers of the traditional medicines. An example is food therapy: people use food to treat and prevent diseases in their daily diet. In some cases, they not only assist each other to gain access to traditional medicines but may also share their experience in using food with therapeutic functions or cook food for each other for this purpose.

Social Inclusion and Social Exclusion

Social exclusion is a relatively new concept launched at the European level as a practical alternative to the old poverty concept (Levitas, 1998). It is concerned with both distributional and relational issues (Room, 1995). Its increasing importance indicates a growing awareness of the fact that the excluded groups often suffer more than one disadvantage: they may lack sufficient material resources to maintain a decent standard of living as well as lack sufficient opportunities to participate fully in society (Chau and Yu, 2001). Sacaceno (1997) has pointed out: '...If not all the (financially) poor are excluded, not all the excluded are (financially) poor'.

A straightforward way to promote social inclusion is to enable people to gain a socially acceptable standard of living and to participate in mainstream community activities. This can be seen as a way to secure social integration. For example, the European Community tries to cope with social exclusion by helping the socially excluded to obtain paid work. By doing so it expects the socially excluded to use their wages to improve their material quality of life and integrate themselves into society through participation in the labour market (Levitas, 1996).

However, it is important to distinguish between the attempts to promote social inclusion and social control measures. The major difference, we argue, lies in the control over life. Inclusion means not only participating in the mainstream institutions, but also having a degree of control over the form of participation and the decision to take part in the mainstream institutions (Cole, 1999). In fact, it is difficult to say that a person is an active participant if he/she is forced to take part in mainstream activities. That is why some analysts such as Townsend (1997) and Walker (1997) propose measures to redistribute resources from the rich to the poor in order to reduce social exclusion (such as tax reforms and expansion of benefit systems). These measures not only enable the poor to enjoy a socially acceptable standard of living but also give them the choice of living independently of the participation in the capitalist economy as marginal workers. In this sense, a certain degree of autonomy can be seen as a precondition for achieving social inclusion.

In discussing social capital, Woolcock (1998) has introduced the concept of autonomy at both the micro and the macro level. Autonomy at the micro level refers to an individual's looser, extra-community ties or the freedom they have to interact with others outside of their immediate group (linkage). Autonomy at the macro level refers to the capacity of institutions or organizations to act independently, free from the influence of vested interests (integrity) (Hawe and Shiell, 2000). According to the notion of human agency, people have the potential to be active agents in the promotion of self-development, developing social relations, participating in societal activities, meeting both collective and individual ends (Lister, 1997; Gough, 1988). To develop this potential, we should be aware that people may have the capacity to exercise autonomy at both the macro and micro levels whilst seeking social inclusion in the community - that is, they can make extra-community ties and develop principles from which they can act independently of the practices and customs of the mainstream community. In other words, they may be able to achieve both 'linkage' and 'integrity'.

Chinese People's Strategies for Seeking Social Inclusion and Health

Since many Chinese people in Britain are immigrants, in theory they can organise their lives in relation to three communities: the mainstream, the Chinese community in Britain and the community of their origin. To achieve social integration, they can take part in the main activities of these communities. To gain autonomy, they can attach their lives to more than one of these communities or uphold the principles of one community countering those of others. Hence, to promote their health, they have in theory a number of choices, such as:

(a) to use western medicines provided in Britain;
(b) to use Chinese medicines (both formal and informal) provided in Britain;
(c) to use western medicines provided in their place of origin;
(d) to use Chinese medicines (both formal and informal) provided in their place of origin;
(e) to use different types of medicines at the same time.

Since different treatments and medicines are characterised by different fundamental philosophical and behavioural dimensions, choosing which medicines to use often involves choosing the related framework and concepts to understand the disease or illness (Wilkinson and Sussman, 1987). Hence, it is feasible for Chinese people to rely on different theoretical frameworks and principles underpinning different medical systems to promote their health. It is also possible that they use one principle against another so as to achieve integrity.

For example, Lee's study (1981) has found that Chinese people in Mainland China have mixed feelings towards western medicine. While they are willing to take western medicines in the belief that they are effective in dealing with acute disease, they judge the side-effects based on their traditional knowledge. Traditionally, western medicines have been regarded as 'cold' in property and were thought to disturb the 'cold-hot' balance of the body (these traditional medical concepts will be discussed in the following section). As a result, many Chinese people see western medicines as only a short-term solution to their diseases and prefer Chinese medicines in the longer term. Koo (1984) has also discovered that Hong Kong Chinese classify food (including western food such as fish oil) according to their traditional medical framework. Such a classification not only helps them to decide whether to accept the western foods, but also defines how the food can be used.

Moreover, all these choices for promoting health inclusion with the emphasis on integration, linkage and integrity are associated with the different types of relationship between suppliers and other users of medical services. For example, if Chinese people in Britain want to achieve social integration in promoting health, they would use western medicines and would need to establish an effective patient-doctor relationship with the mainstream medical practitioners. However, if they want to achieve linkage, they would use more than one type of medicine in Britain, or the same type of medicine in more than one community (such as the mainstream in Britain and Hong Kong). This may cause competition between different medicines or between the same type of medicine in two places. If Chinese people want to enhance integrity, they would use the principles of one type of medicine to counter the principles of the other. Such an attempt may enable them to shorten the social distance between themselves and the suppliers of one type of medicine but may keep the suppliers of another type of medicine at a distance.

However, it is one thing to state the theoretical possibilities of achieving social inclusion; it is quite another to have the opportunities to turn them into reality. Whether the choices mentioned above can be turned into reality depends on various factors, including cultural factors, pragmatic considerations and the effects of globalisation.

Factors Affecting Chinese People's Strategies for Seeking Social Inclusion and Health

Cultural factors

China is a vast country and has a long history. Its civilization has lasted a number of millennia. One of the important tasks that each generation has to tackle is how to overcome everyday problems whilst at the same time maintaining the cultural identity by sharing the cultural heritage, of which traditional medicine is an indispensable part.

Lee (1981) has classified Chinese medicines into two categories: the great traditions (formal medicines) and small traditions (informal medicines). The great traditions emerged in China in about 800 BC. They are based on the cosmological conception of Yin-Yang and the Five Elements, the functions of '*qi*' (flow of energy), blood, mind, essence and body fluids, as well as their relationship to each other (WHO, 1999). The main examples are herbal medicine and acupuncture, which were formalised in traditional Chinese society.

Since formal medicines were very expensive, most people relied on informal medicines such as religious healing and food therapy to cure disease and to promote their health. Although the way in which the informal medicines were used varied from one community to another, depending on the community's shared experience and the type of resources available, people tried to link their small traditions to the great traditions in several ways.

Firstly, people always tried to find a theoretical basis for informal medicines from the formal medicines. For example, both the rationale and philosophy of food therapy are derived from the ideas of practitioners of formal medicines. Cou Xuan, a famous Chinese physician, has formally supported the use of food therapy and related it to the concepts of Yin and Yang:

> Physicians must first recognize the causes of an illness and know what transgression of the normal regular (balance of the Yin and Yang) has taken place. To correct this imbalance, adequate diet is the first necessity. Only when this has failed should drugs be prescribed (quote in Koo, 1984, p 759).

Based on the concepts of Yin and Yang and the belief that the body should be kept at an equilibrium, people further used four additional concepts to classify the functions of different foods and to depict a person's state of health - these are 'hot', 'cold', 'wet' and 'dry'. People shared a common assumption that health can be achieved only when the energy inside the body is in balance. If this balance was disrupted, they might feel 'excessively hot', 'excessively cold', 'excessively wet' or 'excessively dry' (Koo, 1984). To remove these unhealthy conditions, they should not only avoid eating the related types of food but also take food of the opposite nature to restore the equilibrium.

Secondly, people continuously extended the use of the framework in order conceptually to integrate new medicines into the traditional medical systems. As mentioned above, Chinese people use the traditional framework to assess the effectiveness of western medicines and western foods in promoting health.

Thirdly, the public used the same language as the practitioners. Most of them could use the concepts to describe their illnesses to the Chinese medicine practitioners. At the same time as diagnosing the sickness, the Chinese practitioners might also explain the prescription to the patients and advise them to take special types of food (or abstain from certain types of food). Moreover, experienced patients might purchase the medicines without consulting a practitioner if they had suffered a similar illness before.

Constructions of Health and Illness

The techniques Chinese people use to link the great traditions to the little traditions reflect their cultural strategy for seeking social inclusion. They have a tradition of using more than one type of medical system: formal and informal medicines. Moreover, instead of using them separately, they try to link them together by interpreting and reinterpreting the traditional formal framework. By doing so, they not only try to integrate different practices but also try to maintain their cultural identity. These cultural methods of handling alternatives in organising their ways of life also apply to their use of western medicines. This explains why, in our studies, many respondents used Chinese medicine and mainstream medicine at the same time, but used the concepts of the former to interpret the effects of the latter.

Pragmatic considerations

It is important to note that the cultural factor is not the only factor shaping Chinese people's way of organising health. They also consider resources when choosing medical systems to promote their health. In 1949, China had 12,000 western-style doctors (Lee, 1981), but most of them concentrated on delivering healthcare in the urban areas because the people in the rural areas could not afford the western medicines. Furthermore, during the post-war period, the Beijing government has attempted to develop a medical system in rural areas that enlists the help of both western medicine practitioners and barefoot doctors (half-time farmers and half-time doctors who do not have shoes on all the time). Such attempts have been made, largely out of the consideration of saving resources.

Despite an increased awareness of the importance of medical pluralism, biomedicine constitutes the predominant ethnomedical system in Britain, as well as in other European and North American societies (Baer et al., 1997). Its orthodox position is strengthened by a number of factors, such as the medicalisation of people's lives, the government policy which subsidises people to use the biomedicine but not alternative medical systems and the huge amount of money spent on testing and standardising the service quality. This, to a certain extent, explains why alternative treatments are highly under-developed. Hence even if elderly Chinese people in Britain prefer Chinese medicines (formal or informal) to promote their health, they may not find sufficient medicines or practitioners to meet their needs.

Globalisation

Globalisation of the economy also plays a part in shaping people's strategies for seeking social inclusion and health. It has strengthened neo-liberalism, the internationalisation of free markets and the bargaining power of capitalists at the expense of organised labour (Hoogvelt, 1997; Wilding, 1997). These changes have led to further commodification of people's lives and increased the pressure on capitalist governments to provide more investment opportunities, but at the same time reduce expenditure on welfare.

On one hand, the continuous rise in the cost of providing medical services and the increasing demand compel the government to lower the quality of service or force users to share the costs. As a result, people may search for less expensive, yet more effective measures of health care. On some occasions, the government even subsidises people to use alternative medicines. This means it may be possible for Chinese medicines, such as acupuncture, to develop. On the other hand, many alternative medicines, especially the formal treatments, are provided as a commodity. Since lay people may not be able to gain sufficient information on the price and quality of the services before they make decisions, commodification of medical services may make the services more expensive. It may also provide opportunities for suppliers to exploit users' ignorance to make big profits. This is a major reason why some respondents in our study prefer the services provided by GPs to those provided by Chinese medicine practitioners. They regarded the former as more reliable, as the services were part of the National Health Service whilst the latter were more expensive and less reliable as there were no public measures to assure the quality.

Major Findings of the Studies

As mentioned earlier, the discussion within this paper is based on a literature review and the findings of two small studies. Owing to the small size of the samples in the studies, we do not claim that these findings represent the majority views of Chinese people in Britain. However, as shown below, the opinions of many of the respondents' are in line with the literature review above, therefore we believe they reflect, to a certain extent, the pattern of medical pluralism in the daily lives of Chinese people in Britain.

The study of older people in Glasgow

Twenty members of the Wing Hong Elderly Association in the Multi-Cultural Centre in Glasgow were interviewed in this study. They joined the centre's luncheon activities regularly. Four were male and 16 were female. The average age was 69. They all came from Hong Kong and had lived in Britain for more than 20 years. Seventeen had worked in the catering industry and three had stayed at home as housewives since their arrival in Britain. Hakka or Cantonese were their main dialects.

The main aim of the study was to examine the importance of cultural factors in shaping Chinese older people's lives; and to explore whether Chinese older people play an active role in securing social inclusion through building social relationships in both mainstream society and their own community. We focused on their use of food in promoting their health and other factors affecting their health seeking behaviour.

Attitude towards food All the interviewees had used food to tackle health problems and prevent illness. As with Chinese people in traditional China, they used the concepts of hot, cold, wet and dry to analyse their health, and the advantages and disadvantages of different kinds of food to their well-being. An interviewee said: 'It is important to keep our body in balance, free from "excessive heat, excessive cold, excessive wet and excessive dryness".' Another interviewee likens health to personality. She said, 'extreme behaviours originate from bad personality; the presence of extreme syndromes such as excessive heat and excessive cold suggests a poor state of health'.

Interviewees usually dealt with poor health in two ways. The first was to avoid eating those foods which disrupt the equilibrium. The second was to rely on certain types of food and medicine to restore the balance. For example, 17 out of the 20 interviewees believed that excessive heat could be reduced by taking most fruit and vegetables; excessive cold could be counteracted by drinking wine or tonic food, such as chicken soup with Jinseng; excessive dryness could be regulated by syrup soup with sweet potatoes, and excessive wetness could be balanced by certain kinds of herbal tea.

The interviewees also tried to use their traditional framework to judge the advantages and disadvantages of western food. They shared a common view that some western foods such as fish and chips, Coca-Cola and coffee are not healthy because they could cause excessive heat, wetness and dryness respectively. They also felt that western medicines might disrupt the body's equilibrium by causing excessive dryness and cold. They also believed that some 'western' foods could promote their health - for example, celery and salad are believed to be effective in dealing with excess heat. Therefore they did not reject all western food.

Other factors affecting health seeking behaviour From the interviews, it was found that four additional factors affect Chinese older people's health-seeking behaviour. The first concerns their attitude to mainstream medical services. All interviewees expressed difficulties in using mainstream medical services for a number of reasons - the language barrier, difficulties of finding interpreters, failure of medical professionals to understand their traditional health beliefs and the long waiting time. These problems also provide an insight into why respondents relied on their own methods if they thought that the illness was not too serious. However, the majority (17 out of 20) said they would not hesitate to consult GPs if they found that their illness was acute and serious. This is not only because the services are free of charge but also because they believe that western medicine is more effective when dealing with serious illness. Clearly they did not think that the traditional methods could replace western medicines or vice versa. Rather they thought that they were complementary to each other. An interviewee even suggested that GPs should be made aware of this attitude towards western medicines, so that they would recognise that the Chinese patients who seek their help do so out of an urgent need; otherwise they would rely on their own methods.

The second factor is the attitude towards Chinese medicine practitioners. Most interviewees (18) did not want to consult Chinese medicine practitioners when they were ill, despite their belief in the traditional health concepts. The main reason was that the services provided by Chinese medicine practitioners belonged to a commercial system and were not subsidised by the government. Half said that they could not afford to use Chinese medicine practitioners regularly. Eight thought that the services provided by the private market were unreliable. They were afraid that the practitioners might advise them to take more medicine than they needed in order to make more money. An interviewee even thought that the relatively small size of the Chinese population in Britain, compared with Australia, USA and Canada could not attract high quality Chinese medicine practitioners to come and practise.

The third concerns the resources available to the interviewees. As mentioned above, there is a widening wealth gap in the Chinese community. This was reflected amongst the interviewees and it affected their health seeking behaviours. Most of the interviewees lived on benefits (12 out of 20). They promoted their health mainly through their everyday diet. Five occasionally cooked soup with chicken and used some Chinese medicine to deal with their problems of 'excess cold'. Four interviewees, who were apparently economically better off, visited Hong Kong regularly to buy Chinese medicines and Jinseng. One of them occasionally went to Canada for the same purpose. He also asked his friends to send herbal medicines to him from time to time.

The last factor is the interviewees' status in the family. Most of them thought that their traditional methods could be used to promote the health of their family members. However, few of them (only three) were responsible for preparing meals for their family members. Some interviewees (six) mentioned that their grandchildren preferred western foods (such as fish and chips, and Coca-Cola) to the meals prepared by them. Hence they mainly used traditional methods and concepts to promote their own health rather than to look after their family members.

The study of Chinese women in Sheffield

In this study, a questionnaire was sent to 140 members or affiliated members of the Lai Yin Association in Sheffield. Eighty-five valid questionnaires were returned. To counter-check and analyse the findings, ten respondents were invited to discuss the findings in a focus group. The purpose of the study was to explore the health needs of Chinese women and to explore their role and strategies for promoting the health of their families.

Their role in looking after their family's health Most respondents played the role of carer and health provider in the family - 71.8 per cent needed to do housework, 75.3 per cent were responsible for taking care of children and 61.2 per cent performed cooking in their daily activities. Moreover, over one-third of them needed to go out to work; they mainly worked in Chinese take-aways or restaurants.

Most respondents put family issues before their own. When asked to list the things they were worried about, 63.5 per cent mentioned the studies/careers of their children, 60 per cent the health problems of their family members, 52.9 per cent the economic conditions of their family. In the focus group, over half of the respondents (seven out of ten) said that they would feel uneasy and guilty if they were unable to keep their family healthy and financially secure. It is therefore not surprising to see that they were prepared to make sacrifices to prevent these problems, and they believed that other Chinese women would do the same.

The medical systems used by respondents Instead of relying on a single social system or a single medical system to meet their social and health needs, the respondents used a number of different medical systems. These included using Chinese medicine, trying their own methods, buying non-prescriptive drugs from chemists, consulting Chinese medical practitioners, consulting GPs and leaving Britain to seek medical help (e.g. Hong Kong).

Of the respondents 52.9 per cent reported they would consult doctors if they or their family members were suffering a minor illness, more than one third (36.5 per cent) would buy non-prescription drugs from chemists, 22.4 per cent ignored health problems and left recovery to chance, 15.3 per cent took Chinese medicine and 7.1 per cent consulted Chinese medical practitioners.

If they or their family members suffered from serious illness, most respondents chose to consult doctors (80 per cent) and sought help from Chinese medical practitioners (21.2 per cent). However, there were still 11 respondents (12.9 per cent) choosing to ignore the problem and one would leave Britain to seek medical help.

In the focus group, the respondents gave several reasons to explain why they relied on a number of medical systems to meet their health needs. The first is that many Chinese women still use the traditional medical concepts to diagnose their health problems and seek solutions. Some Chinese women believe that certain health problems are caused by adverse elements inside their body. Excessive 'heat' causes muscles to ache and 'wind' trapped inside the body can lead to dizziness. These explanations for their illnesses are widely shared in the Chinese community. However, the respondents thought that western doctors lacked any understanding of these concepts and therefore were not able to help them solve these problems. They also felt that it would be difficult to explain these concepts comprehensively to doctors, even if they could master good English.

Secondly, some respondents believed that different types of medicines were effective in dealing with different illnesses and diseases. This view encouraged them to develop the social capital of linkage in the maintenance and promotion of health – that is they did not rely solely on one type of medicine, and the power of making a choice, in turn gave them certain opportunities to be independent of different medical systems. Despite their complaints about the GPs, lack of understanding of Chinese medicines and the terms used to describe illness, many of the respondents believed that western medicines were much more powerful than the Chinese medicines when treating acute and serious diseases. That is why 80 per cent of respondents would choose to consult a GP rather than a Chinese medical practitioner if their family members suffered from serious illness.

The third reason is related to the different costs and the difficulties involved in using different medical systems. As with other ethnic minorities, many respondents suffered from language barriers and lacked sufficient knowledge of their social rights and the social service system. This prevented them from using the health and medical services effectively. Of the respondents 61.2 per cent thought that their English was either poor or very poor and only 2.4 per cent rated their English as good or excellent. When asked about the difficulties they had come across in using health services, 72.9 per cent of respondents mentioned language barriers. Despite the fact that most of them were members or affiliated members of a women's club, 41.2 per cent said that they did not know that social and health services existed, 45.9 per cent said that they had no knowledge about how to use the services. Moreover, Chinese medicines could be an expensive option to some Chinese people. Since the government did not subsidise consultations with Chinese medicinal practitioners, the respondents needed to pay for any treatment they received. Some respondents also thought there were insufficient rules and regulations to ensure the standard of services provided by the Chinese practitioners.

Conclusion

The paper has discussed the concept of medical pluralism and social inclusion, strategies used by Chinese people to promote their health, and the cultural, global and pragmatic factors influencing their choice of strategies.

The findings of the two studies provide evidence to support the discussion based on the literature review. In securing social inclusion and promoting their health, most respondents attempted to play an active role. Besides attempting to seek a certain degree of integration into the mainstream, the respondents actively tried to secure some autonomy through seeking integrity and linkage. As mentioned above, they used the traditional framework to judge the advantages and disadvantages of western medicines and food. This framework provided them with a guide to retain their cultural identity and the autonomy, to a certain extent, to make choices independently of the mainstream. In addition, some respondents tried to secure certain attachments to different communities by buying foods from other Chinese societies.

Their attempts to secure social inclusion played an important role in shaping their relationship with other users and suppliers of different medical systems. Whilst they occasionally consulted GPs, their relationship with them was by no means close due to language and other barriers. No respondents mentioned any plans to organise users' groups, either with other ethnic groups or with other Chinese people, to strengthen their rights.

While the respondents relied on traditional beliefs to strengthen their health, their relationship with the practitioners of Chinese medicine was also quite remote due to the mistrust created by the commercialisation of the service. They shared their knowledge of food therapy and their feelings about their bodies with other users (potential and actual) and members of their families.

Acknowledgements:

The authors would like to thank Professor Eric Sainsbury and Mr David Phillips for their comments on early drafts.

References

Baer, H., Senjer, M. and Susser, I. (1997), *Medical Anthropology and the World System - A Critical Perspective*, London: Bergin and Garvey.

Cai, J. (1988), 'Integration of Traditional Chinese Medicine with Western Medicine - Right or Wrong', *Social Science and Medicine*, 27(5), 521-529.

Chau, C.M. and Yu, W.K. (1999), *Report on Social and Health Needs of Chinese Women in Sheffield*, Sheffield: Lai Yin Association.

Chau, C.M. and Yu, W.K. (2001), 'Social Exclusion of Chinese People in Britain', *Critical Social Policy*, 21(1), 103–125.

Cole, P. (1999), 'Poverty and Social Exclusion', in N. Richard (ed.), *Ethics and the Market*, pp 117-131, Aldershot: Ashgate.

Congress, E. and Lyons, B. (1992), 'Cultural Differences in Health Beliefs: Implications for Social Work Practice in Health Care Setting', *Social Work in Health Care*, 17(3), 81-85.

Eastwood, K. (1993), 'Primary Health Care', in S. Williams, I. Watt and I.F. Chiu (eds), *Report of a Conference on Chinese Health Care in Britain*, Leeds: University of Leeds.

Elling, R. (1981a), 'Political Economy, Cultural Hegemony and Mixes of Traditional and Modern Medicine', *Social Science and Medicine*, 15(A), 89-99.

Elling, R. (1981b), 'Introduction: Relations Between Traditional and Modern Medical Systems', *Social Science and Medicine*, 15(A), 87-88.

Gallagher, E. and Subedi, J. (1995), *Global Perspectives on Health Care*, Englewood Cliffs, N.J.: Prentice-Hall.

Gough, C. (1988), *Rethinking Democracy*, Cambridge: Cambridge University Press.

Hawe, P. and Shiell, A. (2000), 'Social Capital and Health Promotion: A Review', *Social Science and Medicine*, 51, 871-885.

Hoogvelt, A. (1997), *Globalisation and the Post Colonial World: The New Political Economy of Development*, Basingstoke: Macmillan.

Janes, C. (1999), 'The Health Transition, Global Modernity and The Crisis of Traditional Medicine: The Tibetan Case', *Social Science and Medicine*, 48(12), 1803-1820.

Koo, L. (1984), 'The Use of Food to Treat and Prevent Disease in Chinese Culture', *Social Science and Medicine*, 18(9), 757-766.

Kroeger, A. and Franken, H. P. (1981), 'The Educational Value of Participatory Evaluation of Primary Health Care Programs: An Experience with Four Indigenous Populations in Ecuador', *Social Science and Medicine*, 15(B), 535-539.

Lee, R. (1981), 'Chinese and Western Medical Care in China's Rural Commune: A Case Study', *Social Science and Medicine*, 15(A), 137-148.

Leslie, C. (1980), 'Medical Pluralism in World perspective', *Social Science and Medicine*, Vol.14B, 191-195.

Levitas, R. (1996), 'The Concept of Social Exclusion and the New Durkheimian Hegemony', *Critical Social Policy*, 16(1), 5-20.

Levitas, R. (1998), *The Inclusive Society? Social Exclusion and New Labour*, Hampshire: Macmillan.

Lister, R. (1997), *Citizenship: Feminist Perspectives*, Hong Kong: Macmillan.

Parker, B. (1988), 'Ritual Co-ordination of Medical Pluralism in Highland Nepal: Implications for Policy', *Social Science and Medicine*, 27(9), 919-925.

Phillips, D. and Saul, R. (1999), 'Ghosts and Germs: Cerebral Palsy in Nepal, a Preliminary Exploration of Cosmology and Disability', in E. Stone (ed.), *Disability and Development*, pp. 210-227, Leeds: Disability Press.

Room, G. (1995) (ed.), *Beyond the Threshold: Measurement and Analysis of Social Exclusion*, Bristol: The Policy Press.

Sacaceno, C. (1997), 'The Importance of the Concept of Social Exclusion', In W. Beck, L. Maesen and A. Walker (eds), *The Social Quality of Europe*, pp 157-164, London: Kluwer Law International.

Stone, L. (1976), 'Concepts of Illness and Curing in a Central Nepal Village', *Contrib. Nepal. Stud.*, 55-80.

Streefland, P. (1985), 'The Frontier of Modern Western Medicine in Nepal', *Social Science and Medicine*, 20(11), 1151-1159.

Townsend, P. (1997), 'Redistribution: The Strategic Alternative to Privatisation', in A. Walker and C. Walker (eds), *Britain Divided: The Growing Truth of Social Exclusion in the 1980s and 1990s*, pp 263-278, London: CPAG.

Walker, A. (1997), 'Introduction: The Strategy of Inequality', in A. Walker and C. Walker (eds), *Britain Divided: The Growing Truth of Social Exclusion in the 1980s and 1990s*, pp 1-16, London: CPAG.

Watt, I.S., Howel, D. and Lo, L. (1993), 'The Health Care Experience and Health Behaviour of the Chinese: A Survey Based in Hull', *Journal of Public Health Medicine*, 15(2), 129-136.

WHO (1999), *Guidelines on Basic Training and Safety in Acupuncture*, Geneva: WHO.

Wilding, P. (1997), 'Globalisation, Regionalism and Social Policy', *Social Policy and Administration*, 31(4), 401-428.

Wilkinson, D. and Sussman, M. (1987), 'Medical Pluralism in the Twentieth Century', *Marriage and Family Review*, Vol. 11, no. 3(4), 1-9.

Woolcock, M. (1998), 'Social Capital and Economic Development: Toward a Theoretical Synthesis and Policy Framework', *Theory and Society*, 27, 151-208.

Yu, W.K. (2000), *Chinese Older People; A Need for Social Inclusion in Two Communities*, Bristol: Policy Press.

Chapter 6

Shifting Views of Depression: Analysing People's Accounts of their Suffering

Ilka Kangas

Introduction

How do people conceive of depression in contemporary European societies that are said to be characterised by individuality, risks and plurality of values and information? The starting point of this article is that accounts of depression reflect the social and individual pressures people encounter (Kangas, 2001) and people's views of depression thus also describe the society. The aim of this article is to analyse these views with the help of illness accounts told by Finnish people suffering from depression.

Physically, European people are healthier than ever. Hence, it is not surprising that psychosocial factors have been argued to be the limiting component of the quality of life once a certain level of material wealth has been reached (Wilkinson 1996). This brings into question the biographical, cultural and social conditions on which health is based. Depression is one of the phenomena reflecting the psychosocial environment people now live in: during the twentieth century, its prevalence has increased twentyfold (Healy, 1997).

Our era, late modernity, has been associated with corrosive effects of increasing complexity, individualisation and risks (e.g. Williams, 2000; Bury, 1998; Beck, 1992; Giddens, 1991). In these circumstances, life has become a task and a labyrinth, and people's feelings of stress, anxiety and dilemmas of insecurity increase (Bauman, 1999). Richard Sennett (1997), in his powerful critique of the so-called flexible society and new capitalism, notes that, as a consequence, people's emotional lives are adrift. It has also been suspected that as part of the late modern condition, psychosocial welfare of people has become complex and more difficult to reach (e.g. Williams, 2000). The fact that depression has become a major public health problem in the western world is a sign of this tension between individuals and society, not only a sign of mental illness or intrapsychical problems.

Depression is said to be the common cold of psychiatry, *the* mental illness (e.g. Busfield, 1996). Yet there are a variety of views of what constitutes depression (e.g. Pilgrim and Bentall, 1999), depending on the discipline, perspective and interests. Medical understandings of depression can roughly be divided into neurochemical explanations and more psychoanalytic, in other words intrapsychological and intersubjective, views that stress losses and adversities as triggering events (e.g. Healy, 1997). Often depression is presented as a syndrome, comprising both emotional, psychomotor and somatic disturbances (Pilgrim and Bentall, 1999, 233). It is against this backdrop of multiplicity of views that I set out to investigate peoples' views of depression.

With medical and psychological theories readily available, people's health and illness views contain information of these and other expert knowledge bases (e.g. Adamson, 1997; Hunt et al., 1989); they also contain other cultural understandings. People also hold varying views of professional expertise (e.g. Pilgrim and Bentall, 1999). It should be noted that because of increased media coverage and health information, more and more medical knowledge has become common sense (see also Radley 1994) and is discussed when people reflect their illnesses. Medical information and terminology have become a part of people's epistemology and form a part of the resources in making sense of illness and health. Yet health and illness are profoundly social and cannot be fully comprehended from a medical perspective. The culture and society people live in deeply shape the understanding and experience of illness.

An increase of stress was common among Finnish employees during and after the economic recession in the early 1990s. Fear of unemployment and overworking make a vicious circle easily leading to burnout. Stressful events or conditions such as economic worries or conflicts in family or work relations are especially common among the younger generations: In 1997, 32 per cent of 22-34-year-olds reported economic problems, 29 per cent had constant work pressures and 19 per cent reported depressive symptoms. (Luoto et al., 1999.) In 2000, 28 per cent of the Finnish 15-24 year old females reported having experienced depression in the past month (Helakorpi et al., 2001). At the clinic of the University Student Health Care Foundation (YTHS) in Helsinki the rate of visits to a GP because of depression has increased by 50 percent since 1999 (Paavola, 2002). Depression and other mental health problems are also the commonest cause of early disability retirement (www.elaketurvakeskus.fi/suomi/tilastot).

In Finland, depression has slowly become a more acceptable illness, no longer as negatively stigmatised as ten or 15 years ago. Newspapers frequently report on depression morbidity figures and discuss medication, marginalisation and work disability. Magazines interview celebrities and experts and sometimes also lay people suffering from depression. Self-help groups have been founded and web pages containing tests to discover depression have multiplied. The ailment has been named one of the major threats to public health, much like other post-industrialised countries (e.g. Healy, 1997), and the problem of underdiagnosing has been brought under attention, although without any reflection of the role of pharmaceutical industry in promoting the problem (e.g. Healy, 1997). The media presents a 'normalising' view of depression: it is described as an everyday problem, devastating yet curable, that anybody could fall ill with. Magazine articles contain coping or survival stories, narratives of suffering and healing. Talk of a melancholic folk character, so popular for example in the analysis of Finnish alcohol consumption habits, is almost non-existent. In this context, it is now much easier to discuss depression and seek help.

Subjects and Methods

The data consist of two small sets of interviews conducted in order to explore how people suffering from depression interpret and experience their illness. All subjects were recruited on the basis of self-reported depression. They were asked to describe their illness, what they thought of depression, how they perceived of and defined it and how they coped with it.

The first set of interviews was conducted with adults, both men and women, in the capital area of Finland. Eleven subjects, aged 36-56, were interviewed; three of them were male and eight female. The subjects varied in education and profession from journalist and project manager to ex-farmer, pensioner and secretary. The majority, however, were originally from upper or lower middle class backgrounds. Subjects were found with the help of two mental health organisations and their members' networks.

The majority of these subjects had received a diagnosis of depression but the duration of their illness varied from a suspected onset in childhood to three years of distress caused by depression. The severity of depression of the interviewees also varied. Five of the subjects had gone through episodes of institutionalisation because of depression. Not all of the subjects had agreed to take medication for their depression but some had tried several brands. All except one had also tried some form of counselling or psychotherapy.

The second set of interviews was conducted with eight 20-29 year old university students, also in the capital area of Finland. Subjects were reached through students' associations. A request to contact the study was placed on these associations' e-mail lists and, perhaps not surprisingly, only women replied to the request. This could limit the comparison of the two sets of data but also reflects the fact that more women than men report depression (e.g. Busfield, 1996). The comparison of the illness accounts of the two groups is, nevertheless, not complex because of the female majority in the adults' group.

The onset of depression among the female students varied from teenage to recent months. One of the subjects had been in a hospital after a suicide attempt. Five of the young subjects had at some point tried antidepressants and seven had also tried various forms of therapy or counselling.

At the beginning of the interview, all subjects were asked to tell the story of their depression. More detailed questions concerning the experience and meaning of depression were asked at the end of the interview. Subjects were also asked about the effects and consequences of their disorder. For the purposes of this article, the perceptions of depression expressed in the illness accounts were analysed, and causes of, and reasons for, depression were reviewed and compared in order to find out how people explain and view their depression.

Generational Similarities and Differences

There is a generational difference between the adult subjects and these young women. A generational distinction can also be noticed in the perceptions of depression. It is noteworthy that the accounts of men in the adult group did not differ from the accounts of women: they used the same explanations of their depression. Thus, gender in this small sample of depressed people did not seem to make a difference in how people view depression.

The adults' accounts of depression contained a lot of suffering; disappointments, losses, adversities, traumatic experiences and other problems were presented as the causes of depression. Because a detailed analysis of these depression narratives has been presented elsewhere (Kangas, 2001), it suffices to say that three types of explanations following a distinctive storyline were detectable: firstly, an explanation concentrating on the shortcomings or deprivations of early development, focusing on childhood and adolescence experiences. This explanation can be termed *psychological*: it echoes popular and somewhat superficial psychological theories and explanations of depression although in individualised and personified forms. A second explanation was formed along precipitating and symptom-provoking factors in adulthood, outlining a story of hardships, losses and other severe life events, which were reacted to with depression. A third explanation focused on excessive demands and role-conflicts, presented as causes of work-related burnout that developed into, or already contained, traits of depression. These two explanations are more *social*, reflecting the relevance of social conditions, life trajectories and societal demands to depression. Five interviewees talked extensively about changes and problems of society in relation to depression. It is noteworthy that a *biomedical*, neurochemical explanation was mentioned only a few times in the adult interviews and even then often in passing.

Often the account of depression contained several explanations, reflecting upon different causes of the condition. A few of the subjects presented a *holistic* explanation of depression, combining psychological, social and other explanations. This reflects the fact that an illness is often an indeterminate process that cannot be represented from a single perspective (Good, 1995).

As an example of the many-sidedness of depression accounts, let us take the case of 'Maija', a 53-year-old computer operator, who has retired because of depression. Five years earlier she suffered from work-related burnout that soon uncovered depression. In the interview, she recounted other significant episodes of her life during that period, all having a negative impact on her mood. She had recently lost her mother and fallen ill with adenoma, which 'affected her womanhood'. Her marriage was already deteriorating and when her husband didn't understand her depression they finally got divorced. Within two years this previously energetic woman had been forced to an early retirement due to the disability depression had caused. She gave several explanations to her depression, reflecting on her loss of creativity at work, the many adversities of her social and family life, her physical illness and childhood environment. 'I have realised that many things have predisposed me to depression. There have been physical and emotional issues. – I've also learned to look for past events, childhood, that bear relevance'. She presented a rather critical social view by stating that depression is 'in a sense an illness of the welfare society. It is an advanced reaction to change and loss. Our present society is busy and efficient, concentrating on performance. Depression forces people to stop and think and adjust in a situation where there isn't time'. She also worried that the real limits of individual endurance can be crossed: 'One is supposed to heal quickly and fast or move aside and tolerate it. – I wonder if depression is a self-defence mechanism or is it a reaction? Is it good or bad and where does the border lie? Is it a way of acting healthily or as ill? Of that I'm not sure.'

The adult depression accounts shared the characteristic of having an external view of the etiology of depression: the subject was not responsible for falling ill with depression, nor was s/he capable of resisting it. Rather, the sufferer had involuntarily and unwittingly been exposed to circumstances and conditions that would cause anyone to be depressed. The moral position of the subject was that of a victim, and self-infliction was thus ruled out as an alternative (Kangas, 2001). In describing their depression, the subjects used both psychological, social, holistic and occasionally medical explanations. The storyline was, nevertheless, clearly emphasising the importance of social situations that lead into suffering and depression. Only one of the adult interviewees suggested that personality or character could have something to do with the onset of depression. This interviewee was the youngest of the adult group and a student herself.

The view of depression among the female university students was slightly different. They also explained their depression with childhood deprivations and later provoking events and circumstances, and also with stress overload, sometimes combining these explanations. The biomedical explanation was also more popular among the young subjects than among the adults.

There was, however, a fifth explanation, outlining depression as a *personality trait* of inner making, that characterised the students' accounts. Six of these eight young women partly blamed their character for their depression.

Although women students reflected several explanations for their depression and used different cultural resources in defining it, the conspicuous feature of their descriptions was the relationship of experiences, emotions and everyday life to depression. Depression was triggered by lack of motivation or interest, uncontrollability of situations, harriedness, inability to plan the future, meaninglessness, self-disgust, low self-esteem, pessimism, insecurity, unhappiness, anxiety, feelings of emptiness and disappointment in daily life or relationships.

Consider 'Nina', a 24-year-old student of social sciences. She encountered depression after she had been selected as an executive for an international student organisation. She had had a predecessor whom she highly respected and set as her role model. She said that 'I tried to be as her but it didn't work out since I'm different. When I constantly compared myself with her I constantly failed'. Her analysis of the situation goes as follows:

> I set too high targets too soon, so high I had no way of reaching them and then I got depressed and frustrated, because I simply expected too much of myself and I felt that other people did that too and I was not appreciated for what I am.

She reacted strongly to her assumed failure:

> I spent nights awake, I got into a vicious circle of not sleeping. I fell asleep in the evening but woke up at three and couldn't sleep anymore. I slept two hours per night and it was the first time that stress got to me, I didn't know how to work, I couldn't perform. I used to enjoy a little sense of urgency but now I didn't meet my deadlines'. 'I totally lost my ground, I didn't know who I was, what I wanted, what I should do –I was totally lost.'- 'I went really down mentally, sometimes I contemplated suicide, I wondered how I could get out of the situation because nobody wanted or needed me, I mean that I had no self-respect and my performance deteriorated.

> I knew I had no reason to be depressed, everything was supposed to be fine so why did I feel so miserable. I mean I had an intriguing job, I had lots of people around. Why on earth did I feel so lousy, *I must have been the one to blame* [italics IK], because I had no reason to be unhappy.

Nina and her cosufferers seem to experience their social milieu as demanding, unsettling and even overwhelming. 'We are expected to be perfect leaders or executives instantly', she commented. It has been proposed that the flexibility market capitalism demands of people is hard to tolerate. A continual worry or vulnerability in the face of changes, risks and speculative markets makes rational decision-making and social orienting difficult (Sennett, 1997). A 27-year-old student voiced this even more strongly: 'You are expected to be ever so strong and capable and able yet the competition in this society just increases all the time. Perform, perform, you can do better – but you can't.' The 'prisoners of the present' find no solution, no escape – hence depression.

The adult subjects described their relationship to their social milieu – also sometimes containing a sense of overwhelmingness, but much more often suggesting that their *lifecourse*, its circumstances and events, had been too difficult to bear or that they had encountered too many adversities and thus became depressed. These young women, on the other hand, had come to a conclusion that also they *themselves*, not only their lives or its conditions, were the ones to blame for depression. 'I would describe it as a personality trait. – it is a way to behave.' 'I'm a moody person. – I've had it so long that it is a part of my character.' This inward turn, taking blame and responsibility, has taken place in a situation where influence on structural conditions seems to be beyond the reach of the suffering individuals.

This internalised view of causes of depression would be rather gloomy, were it not contradicted in some of these young women's talk with the broader, more general causes of depression, by which they show an awareness of the state of society they live in. 'I think depression is a deficiency syndrome of society' commented one of the young women, elaborating her view by mentioning the increasing frequency of mental health problems of employed people and by suggesting that not enough attention is paid to peoples' emotional wellbeing. There is, however, bitterness and disappointment in some of the remarks: 'If happiness is so hard to reach it is not worth it', said a 22-year-old student of biology. This awareness of depression as a consequence of societal conditions was mentioned, however, only by the minority of the young interviewees.

In some of the accounts of depression by the younger subjects, depression was also being normalised. 'It is a way to look at the world', commented a 29 year old student. 'I don't think there is anything to be afraid of, it is just a part of ordinary life', said a 26-year-old. These neutral views express a relative perspective: feeling low is a part of life.

It seems that both groups of interviewees share a view of depression invoked by early or later losses, pressures and adversities of the life course. At the same time, the younger subjects take more responsibility and express more fatalism than the adult subjects.

Conclusions

Although this study focused on a limited number of depression accounts, it raises several questions that carry more general relevance. Subjects of this study made sense of their illness by using several cultural resources, such as expert knowledge and media images, in order to describe and explain their own personal experience. Personal illness experience is explained to others with the help of shared cultural resources (Herzlich, 1973; Fife, 1994) and expert knowledge is clearly one of the resources although not the only one. In these illness accounts, depression is presented as a social and personal problem restricting and disabling the social and personal lives of the sufferers. Some of the subjects expressed critical views towards society for inflicting depression. The more internalised and intrapsychical views the young women voiced are still alarming; they suggest a disempowerment and detachment of individuals in relation to the social determinants of depression. Worries have, indeed, become more private (Bauman, 1999). On the other hand, if depression is also becoming normalised among the young, it can make it less difficult to tolerate; everybody feels melancholic sometimes and the sufferer is thus not isolated (see Karp, 1996 for this main characteristic of depression).

The concept of depression in psychiatry has been criticised for being insufficiently broad to cover oppressive social and political factors contributing to human suffering (Pilgrim and Bentall, 1999). Yet some of these people describe depression also as an ailment caused by the society. Wolf Lepenies (1992) has argued that melancholy is a reflection of a class-wide sense of powerlessness and uselessness. Following his line of thought, it could be asked if a growing number of people, especially from the middle classes, are becoming marginal in their own society? The increasing (sense of) responsibility and reflexivity of the individuals lead to situations where many social problems are interpreted as something that can, and should, be solved through personal action at an individual level (Abrahamsson, 1999) and the responsibility of failure seems to fall on the individual (Bauman, 1999). When situations become privatised in this way, people are at loss with the effect of societal changes in their personal lives (see also Sennett, 1997).

People are increasingly aware of the growing number of discontinuities, uncertainties and risks, whether economic, social or emotional, in their lives. The expectations of a stable and progressive life have diminished and insecurity has replaced confidence. Stripped of firm prospects (Bauman, 1999), precariousness is the common feature especially of young adults' life conditions. Within the context of market promises of the perfect and instant life, the flow of ordinary life with its adversities, disappointments and arbitrariness increasingly promote confusion and discontentment. Especially among the younger generations, depression seems to become an almost natural way to react to this distress. At the same time, depression has become *the* expression of the situation, of the difficulties of living in the era of late modernity.

It seems that welfare states and market economies do not necessarily produce content citizens but agonised individuals who tire in the face of the complex society. The consumer culture with its instantaneousness of desires, late modernity with its emphasis on individuality and concentration on the self lead into a tragedy of the unattainable: success, health, wealth, fitness, beauty, satisfaction and happiness are assumed but understandably not all reached, bringing forth disillusionment, detachment or extensive pressure to perform even better. It is as if the information society could not provide its individuals with insight or ability to lead a reasonably content life. Rather, younger generations seem to be armed with a weakening sense of strategic agency. When ordinary life seems to become too arduous to bear, and it is reacted to with depression, it suggests serious problems within society, not necessarily, or only, within or between individuals.

References

Abrahamsson, P. (1999), *The Scandinavian Model of Welfare in Comparing Social Welfare Systems in Nordic Europe and France*, Nantes: Mire Drees collection.

Adamson, C. (1997), 'Existential and clinical uncertainty in the medical encounter: an idiographic account of an illness defined by inflammatory bowel disease and avascular necrosis', *Sociology of Health and Illness*, 19, 133-159.

Bauman, Z. (1999), *Liquid Modernity*, Oxford: Polity Press.

Beck, U. (1992), *Risk Society: Towards a New Modernity*, London: Sage.

Busfield, J. (1996), *Men Women and Madness. Understanding Gender and Mental Disorder*, London: Macmillan.

Bury, M. (1998), 'Postmodernity and Health', in Scambler, G and Higgs, P (eds), *Modernity, Medicine and Health. Medical Sociology Towards 2000*, London: Routledge.

Fife, B. (1994), 'The conceptualisation of meaning in illness', *Social Science and Medicine*, 38, 309-316.

Giddens, A. (1991), *Modernity and Self-Identity. Self and Society in the Late Modern Age*, Cambridge: Polity Press.

Good, B. (1995), *Medicine, Rationality and Experience. An Anthropological Perspective*, Cambridge: Cambridge University Press.

Healy, D. (1997), *The Antidepressant Era*, Cambridge: Harvard University Press.

Helakorpi, S., Patja, K., Prättälä, R. and Uutela, A. (2001), *Suomalaisen aikuisväestön terveyskäyttäytyminen ja terveys*, kevät 2001 (Health behavior and health of Finnish adults), Helsinki: Kansanterveyslaitoksen julkaisuja B 16/2001.

Herzlich, C. (1973), *Health and Illness. A Social Psychological Study*, London: Academic Press.

Hunt, L., Jordan, B. and Irwin, S. (1989), 'Views of what is wrong: Diagnosis and patients' concepts of illness', *Social Science and Medicine*, 28, 945-956.

Kangas, I. (2001), 'Making sense of depression: perceptions of melancholia in lay narratives', *Health*, 5: 76-92.

Karp, D. (1996), *Speaking of Sadness. Depression, Disconnection and the Meanings of Illness*, Oxford: Oxford University Press.

Lepenies, W. (1992), *Melancholy and Society*, Cambridge: Harvard University Press.

Luoto, R., Helakorpi, S., and Uutela, A. (1999), *Lama ja terveys* (Economic recession and health). Aikuisväestön terveyskäyttäytyminen (AVTK)- aineiston 7-vuotisseurantatutkimus 1989/90- 1997, Tutkimuksen toteutus ja perustaulukot. Helsinki: Kansanterveyslaitoksen julkaisuja B10/1999.

Paavola, A-L. (2002), 'Masentavaa? YTHS:n johtajaylilääkäri Marja Niemen haastattelu' (Depressing? An interview with the chief physician Marja Niemi from the University Students Health Foundation), *Yliopisto-lehti*, 6:24-25.

Pilgrim, D. and Bentall, R. (1999), 'The medicalisation of misery: A critical realist analysis of the concept of depression', *Journal of Mental Health*, 3:261-274.

Radley, A. (1994), *Making Sense of Illness. The Social Psychology of Health and Disease*, London: Sage.

Sennett, R. (1997), *The Corrosion of Character. The Personal Consequences of Work in the New Capitalism*, New York: W.W. Norton.

Wilkinson, R. (1996), *Unhealthy Societies: the Afflictions of Inequality*, London: Routledge.

Williams, S. (2000), 'Emotions, social structure and health. Rethinking the class inequalities debate', in Williams, S.J., Gabe, J. and Calnan, M. (eds), *Health, Medicine and Society. Key Theories, Future Agendas*, London: Routledge.

Chapter 7

The Construction of Lay Resistance to Vaccination

Pru Hobson-West

Introduction

Vaccination, in terms of both science and public policy, is undoubtedly an international issue. For example, a debate is going on about the relationship between vaccination and aid (Fleck, 2002), and around vaccination strategies and the threat of biological warfare, particularly after September 11 (Bicknall, 2002; Fauci, 2002). Since the 2001 foot-and-mouth disease outbreak in the UK, vaccination of livestock has also hit the headlines, with recent warnings from the EU that vaccination, rather than mass slaughter may be deemed compulsory in the event of a future outbreak. However, the discussion here focuses on the UK and mass childhood immunisation (MCI).

Immunisation, and MCI in particular, is usually presented as one of the greatest success stories of modern medicine. Lay resistance to vaccination has thus been regarded as puzzling by many inside and outside the medical profession. Health education literature discusses vaccination acceptance in terms of 'uptake', and attempts to offer reasons as to why the Department of Health's aim of 95 per cent coverage is not always being met (Hey, 1998, p. 1). The importance of the attitudes and enthusiasm of health professionals is stressed, along with the influence of factors such as ease of access to immunisation services, accuracy of records, and other 'organisational' determinants (see Egan et al., 1994). On a population level, research has found a relationship between uptake and variables such as ethnicity, mobility and socio-economic status (Agbley and Campbell, 1998, pp. 69-73). 'Parental attitudes' is identified as an important category, although this does not seem to have been unpacked or qualitatively researched (although see Rogers and Pilgrim, 1994, 1995).

The aim here is not to offer a full discussion of vaccination uptake, nor is it to predict what proportion of non-uptake is due to 'active' parental opposition versus organisational and structural factors, although this is of obvious interest to healthcare professionals. Additionally, the chapter will not list the arguments for and against MCI (see Nasir, 2000; Poland and Jacobson, 2001; Phillips, 1999). Rather, what follows is based on the assumption that any resistance to childhood vaccination is sociologically and politically significant and deserves analysis as a discourse that has the potential to influence the public and scientific debate on vaccination. The analysis can also help illuminate wider debates within the social sciences on fundamental concepts such as rights, ethics and risk, and help our understanding of differences between lay and medical constructions of health and illness.

The chapter is structured around several interdependent themes that are embedded in the discourse on vaccination. These are: health, disease and prevention; responsibility; risk; and trust and expertise. I would argue that it is only by using these concepts in combination as analytical tools that we can understand the meaning and significance of anti-vaccination and avoid a reductionist portrayal of the controversy as two sides separated only by an information gap (Limoges, 1993). Before getting into the detail, a brief overview of vaccination and anti-vaccination will be provided.

Vaccination and Anti-Vaccination

Vaccination in Britain is usually dated from 1786 with Edward Jenner's first attempt at smallpox vaccination using cowpox legions (Kassianos, 2001, p. 3). The nineteenth century represented a 'long gestation period' for the establishment of a national immunisation programme, during which time the role of the state in public health crystallised (Streefland, 2001, p. 160). Many more vaccines were developed in the twentieth century, including polio in the 1950s and measles in the 1960s. Successive governments of all political persuasions have also continued to invest significant resources in promotion, such as the 2001 £3 million TV campaign (BBC website, 22/01/01).

From 1861, several acts of parliament made smallpox vaccination gradually more enforceable through the appointment of vaccination officers, whose policing led to the fining and imprisonment of individuals who refused (McGuire, 1998, p. 8). Significant protest ensued and a concession was finally granted in 1907 legislation to 'conscientious objectors' (all enforcement measures were withdrawn by 1948). Nineteenth century opposition was mainly an expression of the desire to maintain the boundary between public and private life and to restrict state interference (Porter and Porter, 1988). Even Gladstone spoke of vaccination as an 'attack on "private liberty"' (Beck, 1960, p. 316). In the context of the current heated debate over the safety of the measles mumps and rubella (MMR) vaccine, this historical perspective is useful in highlighting that resistance is as old as the technology itself, and many concerns voiced then are still echoed in twenty first century debates. Objection to vaccination, one could argue, has never just been about disease levels per se, but a complex set of social and political responses to a political issue.

The UK recommended childhood vaccination schedule is similar to other European countries, although the exact timing of immunisations does differ. One feature of 'vaccinology' (Blume and Geesink, 2000) is that although the science is well established, new vaccines and vaccine combinations are being continually developed. Currently, the childhood schedule is: Polio, meningitis C, DTP-hib

(Diptheria, tetanus, pertussis and haemophilus influenzae type b) at 2, 3 and 4 months; MMR at 13 months; Polio, DtaP and MMR at pre-school age; BCG (tuberculosis) at 10-14 years; and diphtheria/tetanus and polio boosters at 13-18 (NHS website).

Although uptake percentages of all of these vaccines are undoubtedly important, especially to policy makers and health service providers, it has been recognised that such statistics are not always sufficient. For example, research has called for improvements in the methods used to record vaccinations (Egan et al., 1994, pp. 75-79). More controversially, recent cases have been documented of vaccine-sceptical parents being struck off GPs lists in order to maintain a surgery's uptake figures and associated financial benefits (Rogers and Pilgrim, 1995, p. 73; BBC website 6/02/02; Scanlon, 2002). In short, practical reasons exist which challenge the notion that vaccination and the success of vaccination policy can be wholly measured through quantitative statistics.

On a more theoretical level, the recent PABE report (2001) on public attitudes to biotechnology argues that 'the relationship between the predominance of public concerns and the intensity of public controversy is not a simple one' (Marris et al., 2001, p. 15). In terms of anti-vaccination research, this warns against an assumed linear correlation between levels of public concern, controversy (beliefs) and vaccine uptake (action). Long-term resentment or opposition could be being fostered even when uptake levels appear high. This mirrors Brian Wynne's argument that the public can feel alienated from an institution (in his case, science), even when this is not shown in open resistance (Wynne, 1993, p. 334). This implies the need for longer-term research on the construction of lay belief on vaccination, and adds justification for research which looks beyond uptake figures.

Health, Disease and Prevention

Vaccination involves the injection of antibodies directly into the body (passive) or, more commonly, the introduction of organisms by mouth or injection which then stimulate the immune system to produce the specific antibodies (active) (Bedford and Elliman, 1998, pp. 2-5). Vaccination is focussed on the community level, so that the level of analysis is the social. According to the ideal of 'herd immunity', however, individuals within the society benefit, as the overall incidence of disease is reduced, if immunisation is maintained at a high enough level. Vaccination is an example of systemic preventive medicine (Mills, 1993), a policy supported as cost effective through standard cost-benefit economic analysis.

A Foucauldian perspective would stress that this simple explanation of vaccination masks the fact that the current dominant understanding of health and disease is a reflection of powerful historical discourses, as opposed to underlying medical truths about the human body (see Annandale, 1998, pp. 34-35). The science upon which vaccination rests is based on the germ theory of disease, the idea that illness is caused by 'foreign invaders' (Bedford and Elliman, 1998, p. 2). A medical anthropology approach is useful here in contextualising this discourse by demonstrating that the expert vision of immunity has changed across time, and can be related to social, as well as scientific changes (see Martin, 1994). More broadly, work in the sociology of knowledge school has also demonstrated that the ideal of 'prevention' itself is culturally constructed (Sachs, 1996). This challenges the assumption that expert understandings are somehow more 'fixed' than lay ones, or that they can be adequately understood without reference to the social or the political.

One explanation for a decline in uptake of vaccination, traditionally given by supporters of mass vaccination, is that the public have a short memory and cannot remember a time when childhood diseases resulted in death and disability (Bedford and Elliman, 1998, p. 1). When individual parents come to make decisions about vaccination their comparison of risk will therefore be biased, as the estimate of the risk of disease, as opposed to the risk of the vaccine, will be artificially reduced. In short, therefore, vaccination is a victim of its own success. Underlying this is the argument that the public have misunderstood the reality of the relationship between health, disease and prevention. The policy implication is that the historical perils of childhood diseases should be advertised, alongside the historical success of vaccination in reducing morbidity and mortality.

What is sometimes forgotten in analyses of contemporary health policies is that they contain assumptions about health, as well as disease. Mass childhood vaccination, resting as it does upon biomedical models, defines health primarily as the absence of disease. However, social scientific research into patients' use of complementary and alternative medicine indicates that other, more holistic, visions of health are becoming more influential (Saks, 1994, p. 85). Homeopathy, for example, has been studied in relation to vaccination resistance (Ernst, 2001; 1999; 1997). Homeopathy conceives of health as something that can continually be improved, where optimum health occurs when all systems – physical and emotional – are in balance. Disease and ill health, therefore, signify imbalance (Gunn, 1992), and take on a highly personal meaning for the individual. By implication, policies designed to educate the public about the dangers of childhood diseases or risk statistics will not convince those who hold a different understanding of the basic categories of health and disease. More importantly, this warns against the assumption that resistance and protest are a *'pure problem of information'* (Beck, 1992, p. 58, original italics), and that more information and education will result in acceptance.

The previous point touches on a broader issue, which has been widely discussed within medical sociology. As already implied, vaccination takes population as the unit of analysis. Epidemiological evidence looks at the incidence of death and disease from a population and translates this into individual risk statistics. Parents are then given a comparison of, for example, the risk of death from measles compared to the risk of death following the MMR vaccine. However, research on other health behaviour (e.g. Purdy and Banks, 2001, part IV) has shown that an individual's health beliefs and decision making does not always conform to mathematical models and is influenced by everyday experience, social networks, and, as Shaw (2002) argues, by the dominant expert paradigm. In other words, lay (and expert) understanding and knowledge of vaccination risks and benefits, like the categories of health, disease and prevention, are socially constructed. Individual resistance to childhood vaccination needs to be understood in this context, and alternative understandings of these basic categories need to be explored.

Responsibility

This section looks at the ethics of vaccination in terms of responsibility. On a basic level, one could argue, vaccination policy makers inevitably occupy a difficult position, as they assume responsibility for the population as a whole, whereas the individual parent only has ultimate responsibility for their own child. More broadly, the pro- and anti-vaccination discourses contain fundamental assumptions and conflicts about where the boundaries of responsibility (and power) lie.

The UK MCI programme is controlled and administered by the state through the National Health Service. Most people, whatever their political leaning, would agree that one of the functions of the state is to protect the weak members of society. Herd immunity is a classic practical example of this, as it ensures that those who cannot be vaccinated (such as children with a weakened immune system), can still be protected (McGuire, 1998, p. 3). On a broader level, one could argue that a modern liberal government has the fundamental democratic responsibility for ensuring a basic level of health and physical mobility. Democracy thus tempers liberalism by demanding democratic rights which the state has a duty to protect (Mills and Saward, 1993, p. 170). The argument is that the demands of positive liberty make preventive health policies (such as vaccination) ethically justifiable, as well as politically and economically desirable.

However, the claim that the state is the ultimate keeper of public health (Streefland, 2001, p. 167) and must act as the responsible agent for the benefit of society as a whole is potentially tempered by the liberal discourse on rights. Immunisation is interesting in acting as a site where individual and community rights appear to conflict and require negotiation. For example, Bradley (1999) discusses the notion that parents have a right to rear their children as they see fit, but that this is often based on the assumption that they will make decisions in the best interest of the child. If parents decide to refuse vaccination then the child's right to receive healthcare, and the community's right to maximum health are being challenged. This argument, of course, assumes that vaccination is in someone's best interest, an assumption which would be contested by those who believe that vaccination is unnecessary. The question is, therefore, not only 'whose rights?' and 'whose responsibility?' but 'whose interests?'.

These broad political questions also have relevance at the level of individual decision making. Without further in-depth qualitative research, it is difficult to make claims about what motivates parents and the extent to which concerns about what is best for society as a whole, or what is considered 'normal', play a part. However, assuming for the moment that social considerations, norms and traditions have influenced vaccination acceptance, increasing reflexivity and individualization (Beck, 1994, p. 7-8) in western society erodes the basis for habit-governed behaviour (Lindbladh and Lyttkens, 2002). Childhood vaccination may thus be increasingly constructed as an important decision (as opposed to an automatic routine or habit) for which the individual parent must take full responsibility. This increases the likelihood that alternative views will be voiced and heard, and that expertise will be questioned. This prediction is supported by Poland and Jacobson who argue that vaccine acceptance is highest in a milieu of 'bandwagoning' (getting vaccinated because it seems like everyone else does) (Poland and Jacobson, 2001, p. 2443).

One explanation for individual vaccination resistance comes from the economic concept of the 'free rider' where an individual, motivated by self-interest, will act to avoid the risk (refuse vaccination), whilst still enjoying the collective benefit of herd immunity (European Commission report, 2001, p. 5). For supporters of vaccination, this is precisely why any expression of anti-vaccination is worrying, as it has the potential to lead to the breakdown of the whole system. The main point to note is that individual resistance to vaccination can be regarded as rational, contradicting the old deficit model of the public understanding of science (PUS), and the assumed lay/rational, expert/rational dichotomy. Indeed, Rogers and Pilgrim have argued that vaccination policy, rather than those who oppose it, should be regarded as the anomaly. Modern health policy is focussed more and more on the idea of healthy lifestyles, where the individual, separate from society, has power to control their destiny and is responsible for promoting health, almost on a minute by minute basis. In this context, 'MCI is anomalous, as it remains fixed on the issue of contagion and the "spaces between people"' (Rogers and Pilgrim, 1995, p. 75) and demands the 'passive acceptance of expert interventions' (Rogers and Pilgrim, 1995, p. 83). This is linked to a wider debate about the role of expertise and trust (see section below).

The last decade has seen a rise in the discourse of public involvement in healthcare and policy decision-making (e.g. The Patients Charter 1991, NHS Plan 2000) and a renewed debate about the need actively to ensure patient consent. In this context, it could be argued that mass vaccination, with its focus on surveillance and a 'fixed regimen' (Greenough and Streefland, 1998, p. 8) does not fit as easily into the new 'medical culture which increasingly places the patient at the centre of decision making' (Annandale, 1998, p. 271).

However, as Rogers and Pilgrim (1995) point out, the government and scientific discourse on mass vaccination is still predominately about uptake, rather than consent. This implies that it is the vaccine sceptics who are identified as the problem. If the public policy aim is simply to maintain uptake, then perhaps it is not surprising that there have been recent calls to make vaccination more compulsory (BBC website 3/07/02), as it is in other countries such as the US (where vaccination is linked to school entry) and France (where it is linked to child benefit payments). Such calls for compulsion are predicted by Misztal's analysis of trust and social order. She argues that if political institutions lose trust, then obedience has to be created through coercion (Misztal, 1996, p. 70). The issue of trust will be discussed further in the final section.

Vaccination and vaccination resistance is covered to some extent in the academic literature on ethics (see Spier, 1998). However, concrete ethical arguments are often disappointingly abandoned in favour of instrumental justification. For example, Bradley concludes 'if the level of population immunity were to fall for a particular vaccine-preventable infectious disease, compulsory vaccination might become a morally justifiable option' (Bradley, 1999, p. 333). Vermeersch uses Mill to argue that coercion is problematic if the aim is to improve someone's wellbeing but *is* justified if the well being of others is in jeopardy. He concludes that compulsory vaccination can therefore be morally justified but still believes that information campaigns, appealing to the 'rational capacities' of people and to their sense of responsibility for others, are preferable (Vermeersch, 1999, p. S17). As will be discussed below, the assumption that information campaigns will be effective as they come from sources that are *trusted* has been called into question.

The previous discussion has assumed that uptake is influenced primarily by individual parents' attitudes to immunisation. However, Health Education Authority and other literature has also focused on the attitudes of health care providers as influential in the parental decision of whether or not to immunise. (Bedford and Kendall, 1998; Chen, 1999). Policy wise, this finding supports the calls for greater training of healthcare staff in arguments both for and against MCI. Clearly, health professionals are important actors in their role as policy implementers, and research into the doctor-patient relationships is relevant here. However, what is also clear is that concentrating solely on vaccination providers as 'champions of vaccines' (Poland and Jacobson, 2001, p. 2441) would be naïve, and risk taking us back to visions of the patient as passive recipient who must simply be encouraged to 'comply'. What this section has demonstrated is that near the surface of the vaccine debate are very difficult questions of ethics and responsibility. It is not the intention to suggest that these questions can be 'resolved', but rather that they must at least be acknowledged by anyone attempting to understand the lay construction of vaccination resistance.

Risk

It is impossible to talk about vaccination or vaccination policy without talking about risk and confronting the vast and growing literature on this concept. On a practical level, this is determined by the fact that the government literature given to parents in doctors' surgeries is organised around risk, and individuals are asked very obviously to compare risk statistics on conditions following the natural disease, with the smaller number of children affected following the vaccine (e.g. Health Promotion England. *MMR. The facts*, 2001).

The pro-vaccination discourse and the medical literature on vaccination take the centrality and relevance of risk as a given. Risk implies that a phenomenon can be measured and can thus be understood as a mechanism for gaining control over a complex reality. The biological factors affecting disease levels and adverse drug reactions (ADRs) are unarguably numerous, but the net result of risk calculations are a neat list of numbers to which everyone, even unscientific parents, can supposedly relate. Extensive research, both in the UK and internationally, is devoted to the production of these risk figures and their dissemination is clearly intended to persuade parents of the rationality of vaccination for their child.

However, even within the mainstream literature has come the realisation that the way that the lay public deals with risk calculations and decisions needs to be examined further. Drawing on social psychology research, risk communication literature has identified the influence of 'media triggers' and 'fright factors' (Bennett and Calman, 1999; Spier, 2001). These do help predict why vaccination is viewed as especially risky; vaccination is about children and the vulnerable, parents have a lack of control over the outcome, the benefits are unclear and difficult to see or quantify, and damage is potentially long term or fatal. Although no doubt influential, this perspective can be criticised for implying that there is an objective reality of risk which the individual has subjectively (emotionally) miscalculated through the inclusion of social and psychological considerations. I would argue, however, that risk, devoid from its social and cultural context, loses most of its meaning.

To continue this thought, I would agree that the debate over vaccination can be used to illuminate social processes, as 'risk debates express contending visions of how society should be organised' (Levidow et al, 2000, p. 190, following Beck). This is because what is classified as a risk and the way that risk is portrayed is a function of the social order, and reflects fundamental assumptions about costs and benefits, and that age-old political question of what constitutes the good life. As Levidow and Carr argue in their analysis of disputes over Genetically Modified (GM) crops, risk assessment only understands a certain type of evidence, which depends on 'worldviews about nature and society ... in seeking and organising more facts about risk, we make socio-political choices' (Levidow and Carr, 2000, p. 260). Sarah Nettleton (1997) goes further to suggest that the concept of risk functions psychologically as a mechanism for gaining control over disease, and is thus a shortcut for confirming our faith in medical science. To describe vaccination as a logical and objective choice through comparing the risk of vaccine damage versus the risk of disease therefore masks the controversial nature of risk itself.

For an example of this social construction, childhood diseases are currently presented as being general risks that are 'out there', which can strike at any time. They are not primarily related to class, gender or other traditional social systems, systems that research in the Engels tradition regarded as key determining factors (Engels, 1844 in Black et al., 1984). Beck and Giddens argue that one consequence of this free floating nature of risk is that risks must be dealt with reflexively, 'as the individual increasingly stands alone, looking for security in the face of uncertainty and an implosion of knowledge systems' (Annandale, 1998 p. 19).

Rather than optimistically assuming that more information promotes empowerment (Annadale, 1998, p. 66), this analysis may help to explain the anxiety felt by the individual who is forced to make a choice as the 'good parent' or the 'responsible citizen', when confronted with a barrage of sometimes conflicting information. This sense of anxiety has come through in the media portrayal of the issues affecting parents making a decision on MMR vaccination

(Allison, *The Guardian*, 7/02/02). An analysis of the political framing of vaccination reveals the tension that Beck and others allude to – between the increasing value placed on individual reflexivity in healthcare, and the moral responsibility of actually making an 'informed' choice (Annandale, 1998, p. 252).

Although the concept of risk has long been part of academic debate, few would deny that there has been a recent 'explosion' (Nettleton, 1997 p. 215) of the concept in sociology and the social sciences, as well as in medical journals. Here is not the place for a substantial review of this literature, although I would like to offer a note of caution in relation to anti-vaccination and the construction of lay beliefs. Given the renewed enthusiasm for the concept it may prove tempting to build aspects of social theory on the back of risk, without empirical justification. In other words, look for risk (and find it), when it isn't necessarily there. As argued, the concept of risk is undeniably central to the expert discourse on vaccination. However, further empirical research is needed to assess whether the public uses risk at all in relation to vaccination decision making, before even beginning to analyse any differences between lay and expert discourses.

Recent European research on public attitudes to biotechnology supports this argument. In relation to GM, the PABE report (2001) argues that it is important not to assume to know the meaning of the debate to the public, and not to assume that we are talking about public perception of *risk*. It may be, in fact, more accurate to talk about 'public perception of uncertainty' (Marris et al., 2001, p. 59). The report also notes that when disagreements cannot be put down to 'risk', policy makers often explain dissent as due to 'other factors'. This 'other' implies reasons which are personal, emotional and non-intellectual (Marris et al., 2001, p. 85). However, it is precisely these 'other' factors that need more research, if we are to improve understanding of how beliefs on vaccination are constructed. If it is indeed the case that the public are interested in the idea of uncertainty and believe that some aspects of disease, health and vaccination are in fact 'unknowable', then policies that continue to focus on risk comparisons or place faith in 'more research' will fail to persuade.

The previous point about the difference between risk and uncertainty deserves clarification. As Wynne argues, a pervasive assumption exists that the public are un-reflexive, demand zero levels of risk and generally have a low tolerance of uncertainty. This is juxtaposed with the portrayal of scientific knowledge as inherently uncertain and science itself as reflexive and 'endemically self-correcting through its intrinsic ability and moral drive to accept scepticism' (Wynne, 1993, p. 323). Following extensive focus group research, the PABE report challenges the 'myth' that the public are incapable of risk comparisons and demand 100 per cent guarantees (Marris et al., 2001, p. 9). This finding adds weight to the argument that lay beliefs on vaccination and vaccination refusal can not be automatically explained away as resulting from a misunderstanding of risk. If attempts to understand lay resistance are simply reduced to this then, I would argue, risk hinders rather than aids the analysis, and the concept becomes corrupted as shorthand for a supposed lay misunderstanding.

Trust and Expertise

The arguments discussed in the sections above are inter-linked to some extent. Ideas about responsibility and ethics are tied up with the notion of the state's role in prevention and health promotion, and notions of risk underlie models of health and disease which justify public health policy. Even more difficult, perhaps, is the separation between trust, risk and expertise.

Trust as a concept is implicit in the pro-vaccination literature, and is mainly hung on the back of the established relationship between doctor and patient. Much of the early work within medical sociology concentrated on this relationship (Blaxter, 2000, p. 1139), and much of value has been learnt about the power relations of the medical encounter. Recent high profile media stories, such as the murder conviction of Dr Harold Shipman and organ retention at Alder Hey and the Bristol Royal Infirmary, have ensured that the notion of trust fills the public and political discourse. The use of trust as *the* concept in this context seems almost unquestioned, as is the assumption that there once was trust, where now there is none (or less).

In terms of vaccination, then, resistance can be explained as resulting from a lack of trust in the professions that are responsible for its administration and promotion. Research in Science and Technology Studies is helpful here, in demonstrating that messages are judged primarily not by content but by source – *'who is telling me this and can I trust them?'* (Bennett and Calman, 1999, p. 4 and see Wynne, 1993). Wynne argues that this is wholly rational as it recognises that as some risks are unknown, the public need to be confident that those in charge will be able to deal with any 'surprises' (Wynne, 2001, pp. 455-456). However, the lack of trust in professions explanation is complicated by UK polls that continually rank doctors as one of the most trusted professions, and have even shown trust rising, despite high profile medical scandals (MORI, 2002). This suggests that the relationship between trust in a certain policy or technology and trust in a profession and its members is complex, and requires further empirical investigation.

To continue this line of argument, science itself can also be seen as one of the (modernist) institutions that legitimises vaccination policy. So, is trust in science falling? Wynne argues that despite claims to reflexivity, science is actually the opposite – and that its lack of openness has encouraged 'public scepticism, alienation and mistrust' (Wynne, 1993, p. 329). This goes back to the previous discussion and the argument that it is perhaps more useful to talk about uncertainty, rather than risk. It also feeds into the debate about whether what is being challenged is expertise itself, an argument to which I will return shortly.

Various groups exist in the UK which contribute to the anti-vaccination discourse, either directly through their campaigns to the public, or indirectly through the media. Each group appears to have a different attitude to vaccination; some arguing against all vaccines, and others sceptical of the safety of certain vaccines or aspects of government policy. A review of their websites supports the need to look at the wider relationships between government, science and the medical profession, a relationship that has been a crucial part of the development of the modern state (Bynum, 1994). Although much space is devoted to competing scientific reports and discussions of the safety of particular vaccines or batch numbers, the institutionalised political relationships are also criticised. For example;

- 'There seems to be a lack of transparency with regard to how vaccine policy is developed and implemented in the UK' (Fletcher, 2001, *JABS*).

- 'Ultimately, the decision whether to vaccinate or not should be based on a logical judgement of the wide spectrum of information available and not on fear, emotional blackmail and the one-sided information available at surgeries. Most GPs have only been presented with the case *for* vaccination and are under immense pressure to toe the official line' (Taylor, 2002, *The Informed Parent*).

- 'Conflicts of interests … the problem is that there is no external-to-the-department scrutiny of such interests, or in the degree of departmental enforcement in practice. Given the major increases in the value of pharmaceutical shares during the 1990s, this appears to be unsatisfactory, particularly in relation to key members of the DoH' [Department of Health] (Thrower, 2001, *Vaccine Awareness Network*).

- 'The doctor…relies on the drug companies' salesmen' to keep him in touch with developments – not the most impartial source in the world!' (*What Doctors Don't Tell You*, 2002).

These issues of regulatory capture (Abraham, 1995) and the 'unholy alliance' of the state and the vaccine industry (Leask and Chapman, 1998) do form part of the anti-vaccination discourse and therefore arguably contribute to a declining trust. If such forces are influential, then government claims that childhood vaccination policy is purely a response to the best independent scientific advice will miss the point. In conceptualising the relationship between government and scientific advice, then, a linear model of knowledge transfer is insufficient. Weingart argues instead for a 'recursive loop', where a problem can be defined by either side, is then passed via political processes back to the scientific community, whose work then redefines the original problem. This forms part of the increasing scientification of politics and the politicisation of science (see Weingart, 1999, p. 157 and responses).

Weingart argues that one consequence of the politicisation of science is that scientific knowledge is appropriated by different political actors, and is then pushed to its limits in the course of the controversy (Weingart, 1999, p. 158). The paradoxical result of this use of science by politics is increasing uncertainty and controversy which contributes to the 'legitimisation crisis for both the scientific expert and the policy-maker that arises out of their interaction' (Rutgers and Mentzel, 1999, p. 146). This approach also helps predict the importance of 'mavericks' in political/scientific controversies, such as childhood vaccination. Dr Andrew Wakefield, whose work has pointed to a link between the MMR vaccine and a certain type of autism (Boseley, *The Guardian*, 2001), has been seized upon as a champion by vaccine sceptical groups, and contributed to the media 'feeding frenzy' over MMR (Spier, 2002, p2847). The fact that the implied policy criticism comes from within the scientific establishment may contribute to the lack of public confidence in present or future scientific advice in confirming or denying a risk (Williams et al., 1995).

To take a broader perspective, perhaps lay concerns about vaccination are best understood not as reactions to a particular policy, or even a consequence of scepticism about particular institutions, but as a result of a lack of trust in all 'expert systems' (Giddens, 1991). This argument follows on from observations about the development of new social movements as 'symptoms of changes in the boundary conditions of the social system', a 'crisis in motivation' (Habermas) or as a result of the failure of traditional institutions of interest mediation (Scott, 1990 p. 7-9). The rise in significance of lay or user groups (Purdy and Banks, 2001, p. 128) and the increasing growth of self-help groups (Kelleher, 1994), should be seen as a critical response to the traditional split between lay and professional understandings of risk, and the perceived rejection by biomedicine of lay concerns and views on health and illness.

Of particular relevance here is the above discussion about the reflexive nature of risk, where individuals are expected to take full responsibility for decisions taken. Trust, if understood as a kind of faith, requires the 'acceptance of the truth of a statement without evidence or investigation' (*The New Oxford Dictionary of English*, 1998). Klein (1995) links the birth of the modern NHS to the post-war consensus and widespread optimism in the progress of medical science. A post-modern perspective would explain current concerns as a breakdown in this consensus and a corresponding breakdown of trust in legitimised authority (Gabe et al., 1994 p. xxii). As Misztal argues, 'the recent increase in the visibility of the issue of trust can be attributed to the emergence of a widespread consciousness that existing bases for social co-operation, solidarity and consensus have been eroded' (Misztal, 1996, p. 3).

These sociological perspectives would all stress the importance of anti-vaccination as social action, even if they disagree on whether or not anti-vaccination should be classified as a 'movement'. The rise of patient groups in the US and UK since the late 1970s is discussed by Wood as evidence of the 'emergence of a more educated and informed population, in which people are accustomed to being treated as consumers rather than patients' (Wood, 2001, p. xii). As patients, they passively accepted that 'doctor knows best' (Ham and Alberti, 2002, p. 839). As consumers, individuals have the capacity and the responsibility to choose – for example in demanding single measles, mumps and rubella jabs. Furthermore, one could argue that the postmodern subject consumes advice and symbols (Barker, 2000, p. 155) as well as concrete products, so that continual trust in one type of expertise is not guaranteed. Alan Petersen argues that the production of the 'at risk self' has meant that there are no longer fixed norms for us to defer to. The 'individual consumer of expert advice can never know for certain whether any particular set of advice is more likely to guarantee security than any other' (Petersen, 1997, p. 202).

To summarise, the concept of trust initially seems to be central to an understanding of vaccination resistance. However, what is less certain is whether changes in uptake figures, the rise of vaccine sceptical groups, and a critical lay and media discourse are best understood as symptoms of distrust. Perhaps other concepts such as faith, responsibility or consent will prove more useful in the analysis. In addition, questions remain about the extent to which anti-vaccination, if it is indeed about trust, is the result of a declining trust in science, a particular government institution, or a more abstract lack of belief in expertise. If the boundary between science and politics is becoming blurred, as implied by Weingart's (1999) analysis, then these dynamics may become more difficult to tease apart.

Conclusion

This chapter has argued that mass childhood vaccination rests on a particular understanding of health and disease. Fundamental political concepts such as rights, and assumptions about the relationship between the individual and society, underlie and justify the policy of mass childhood vaccination. Only by appreciating this can vaccination resistance be understood and potentially addressed. The notions of risk and trust are also useful in framing the debate, but, as this discussion has argued, the meaning and relevance of these ideas *to the public* has sometimes been misrepresented.

The old assumption of the deficit model of PUS implies that providing the public with more facts and information will lead to increasing acceptability, and therefore that individual parents can be educated about the 'rationality' of vaccinating their child. On this reasoning, better training of healthcare providers into the benefits of vaccination and the parental concerns they may face, could also help maintain acceptance. However, by discussing vaccination narrowly in terms of uptake, proponents of vaccination run the risk of simplifying vaccination and individual decision making. Lay parents may hold different or alternative understandings of health and disease causation, some of which may ironically have been encouraged by other state health-care messages, which stress individual responsibility and 'lifestyle' (Petersen and Lupton, 1996).

The reliance of the pro-vaccination discourse on the notion of risk and risk comparisons may also prove to be problematic. The extended use of the term is understandable in allowing a neat mathematical expression of the choices that parents face over vaccination. The desire to conceptualise real changes in the social and economic order in late modernity can also help to explain increased academic interest in the concept of risk and the idea of 'risk society' (Beck, 1992). However, as has been argued, there is nothing inherently rational in adopting behaviour in line with risk statistics. In terms of vaccination and the recent media debate over MMR, it could be that parental concerns can be better discussed using the concept of uncertainty rather than risk.

An analysis of vaccination and vaccination resistance may also illuminate current debates over trust, a concept that is increasingly being presented as a desirable public good or social capital, rather than an automatic by-product of economic processes or regulation (Misztal, 1996, pp. 6-7). This chapter has only touched upon trust debates, but has nevertheless demonstrated the link between public attitude to a technology and trust in legitimising institutions. It has also argued that, in the case of vaccination, the dynamics of this relationship remain unclear and that the evidence available is contradictory. The PABE report argues that the idea that improved communication strategies will resolve the trust issue is a 'misconception' (Marris et al., 2001, p. 11). This is because trust is not simply supported or lost by public relations, and other factors, such as the past behaviour of institutions, are relevant. Indeed, public scepticism may be interpreted as an explicit judgement on the behaviour of the dominant scientific and political institutions, rather than about implicit concepts such as risk (Wynne, 2001, p. 445). If this is so, then the production of more research and information on risk statistics by these very institutions is more likely to exacerbate than allay public concerns.

The lay construction of vaccination is also undoubtedly influenced by experts, and anti-vaccination may partly be understood as significant for expert systems (Giddens, 1991). The division between lay and expert is perhaps less meaningful, at least for those who argue that, in a post-modern society, we are all, to some extent, experts. Paradoxically, this may encourage individual reliance on traditional expert advice, as one of the functions of trust is to provide respite from a complex reality (Misztal, 1996, p. 96). Sometimes, however, expert advice will not be followed or will be problematised, and reliance on more scientific research or more risk education will not succeed, especially if such strategies avoid addressing the complex role of public trust.

This chapter has demonstrated that lay resistance to mass childhood vaccination can best be understood through a multi-layered analysis using the conceptual lenses of responsibility, risk, trust and expertise. More broadly, the anti-vaccination discourse does not arise out of nowhere but is a critical response to the discourse on vaccination, a discourse that must be unpacked to understand better why it is that the debate sometimes seems like a 'dialogue of the deaf' (van Eeten, 1999). As a priority, further investigation is needed to excavate the deeper sources of resistance underlying contemporary concerns about vaccination. Central to this would be an analysis of the nature of public perceptions of the institutions promoting vaccination and, conversely, an analysis of the conceptions of the public employed in health promotion. The science and policy of MCI has always contained assumptions about the meaning of health and illness, meanings based on a certain biomedical model. In short, vaccination has always been about more than expert understanding of disease, just as vaccination resistance is about more than lay (mis)understanding of risk.

Acknowledgements

Doctoral research into the anti-vaccination movement in the UK is being carried out with support from the Leverhulme Trust. Thanks are due to Ian Forbes and Paul Martin for helpful comments on drafts of this chapter.

References

Abraham, J. (1995), *Science, Politics and the Pharmaceutical Industry: Controversy and Bias in Drug Regulation*, University of Reading: UCL Press.
Agbley, D. and Campbell, H. (1998), 'Summary factors affecting immunisation uptake levels', in V. Hey, (ed.), *Immunisation Research: A Summary Volume*, London: Health Education Authority.
Allison, R. (7/02/02), 'Defiant parents stand by decision', *Guardian Unlimited* [online]. Available at http://society.guardian.co.uk/publichealth/story/0,11098,646060,00.html accessed on 7/02/02.
Annandale, E. (1998), *The Sociology of Health and Medicine: A Critical Introduction*, Cambridge: Polity Press.
Barker, C. (2000), *Cultural Studies: Theory and Practice*, London: Sage.
BBC News (22/01/01), £3m to promote MMR vaccine', available at http://news.bbc.co.uk/1/hi/health/1131266.stm, accessed on 29/07/02.
BBC News (6/02/02), 'Child dropped as patient over MMR', available at http://news.bbc.co.uk/hi/english/uk/england/newsid_1803000/1803893.stm, accessed on 6/02/02.
BBC News (3/07/02), 'MMR should be compulsory', available at http://news.bbc.co.uk/1/hi/in_depth/health/2002/bma_conference/2085830.stm, accessed on 29/07/02.
Beck, A. (1960), 'Issues in the anti-vaccination movement in England', *Medical History*, 4, pp. 310-321.
Beck, U. (1994), 'The reinvention of politics: Towards a theory of reflexive modernization', in U. Beck., A. Giddens and S. Lash. (eds), *Reflexive Modernization. Politics, Tradition and Aesthetics in the Modern Social Order*, Stamford, California: Stamford University Press.
Beck, U. (1992), *Risk Society. Towards a New Modernity*, London: Sage.
Bedford, H. and Elliman, D. (eds) (1998), *Childhood Immunisation: A Review*, London: Health Education Authority.
Bedford, H. and Kendall, S. (eds) (1998), *Immunisation: Health Professionals' Information Needs – A Review of the Literature*, London: Health Education Authority.
Bennett, P. and Calman, K. (eds) (1999), *Risk Communication and Public Health*, Oxford: Oxford University Press.
Bicknall, W.J. (2002), 'The case for voluntary smallpox vaccination', *The New England Journal of Medicine*, 346 (17), pp. 1323-1325.
Blaxter, M. (2000), 'Medical sociology at the start of the new millenium', *Social Science and Medicine*, vol. 51, pp. 1139-1142.
Blume, S. and Geesink, I. (2000), 'Vaccinology: an industrial science?', *Science as Culture*, 9, 1, pp. 41-72.
Boseley, S. (2001), 'Doctor's green light for MMR campaign', *The Guardian Unlimited* [online], Available at www.guradian.co.uk/Archive/Article/0,4273,4302476,00.html, accessed on 21/11/01.

Bradley, P. (1999), 'Should childhood immunisation be compulsory?', *Journal of Medical Ethics*, 25, pp. 330-334.

Bynum, W.F. (1994), *Science and the Practice of Medicine in the 19ᵗʰ Century*, Cambridge: Cambridge University Press

Chen, R.T. (1999), 'Vaccine risks: real, perceived and unknown', *Vaccine*, 17, pp. S41-46.

Egan, S., Logan, S. and Bedford, H. (1994), 'Low uptake of immunisation: associated factors and the role of health education initiatives', *Uptake of Immunisation. Issues for Health Educator,*. London: Health Education Authority.

Engles, F. (1844), *Health: 1844*, in Black, N., Boswell, D., Gray, A., Murphy, S. and Popay, J. (eds) (1984), *Health and Disease: A Reader*, Milton Keynes: Open University Press.

Ernst, E. (2001), 'Rise in popularity of complementary and alternative medicine: reasons and consequences for vaccination', *Vaccine*, 20, pp. S90-S93.

Ernst, E. (1999), 'Prevalence of complementary/alternative medicine for children: a systematic review', *European Journal of Paediatrics*, vol. 158, pp. 7-11.

Ernst, E. (1997), 'The attitude against immunisation within some branches of complementary medicine', *European Journal of Paediatrics*, vol. 156, pp. 513-515.

European Commission (2001), *Ethical, legal and social aspects of vaccine research and vaccination policies*, European Commission research project, Psychoanalytic institute for social research, Italy.

Fauci, A.S. (2002), 'Smallpox vaccination policy – the need for dialogue', *Editorial. New England Journal of Medicine*, 346 (17), pp.1319-1320.

Fleck, F. (2002), 'Children's charity criticises global immunisation initiative', *BMJ*, 324, p. 129.

Fletcher, J. (2001), 'Background notes on MMR and late onset autism', JABS website, available at www.jabs.org.uk, accessed on 27/07/02.

Gabe, J., Kelleher, D., and Williams, G. (eds) (1994), *Challenging Medicine*, London: Routledge.

Giddens, A. (1991), *Modernity and Self Identity: Self and Society in the Late Modern Age*, Cambridge: Polity Press.

Gunn, T. (1992), *Mass immunisation: A point in question,* Spark Bridge, Cumbria: Cutting Edge publications.

Greenough, P. and Streefland, P. (1998), 'Social science and immunization', *Items*, 52, 1. New York: Social Science Research Council.

Ham, C. and Alberti, K.G.M.M. (2002), 'The medical profession, the public, and the government', *BMJ*, 324, pp. 838-842.

Health Promotion England (2001), 'MMR. The facts', London: Health Promotion England.

Hey, V. (ed.) (1998), *Immunisation Research: A Summary Volume*, London: Health Education Authority.

Kassianos, C. (2001), *Immunization: Childhood and Travel Health,* 4ᵗʰ edition. Oxford: Blackwell Science.

Kelleher, D. (1994), 'Self-help groups and their relationship to medicine', in J, Gabe., D. Kelleher and G. Williams (eds), *Challenging Medicine,*. London: Routledge, pp. 104-117.

Klein, R. (1995), *The New Politics of the NHS*, 3ʳᵈ ed. London: Longman.

Leask, J-A. and Chapman, S. (1998), 'An attempt to swindle nature. Press anti-immunisation reportage 1993-1997', in *Australian and New Zealand Journal of Public Health*, 19, pp. 17-26.

Levidow, L. and Carr, S. (2000), '"Unsound science?" Transatlantic regulatory disputes over GM crops', *International Journal of Biotechnology*, 2 (1/2/3) pp. 257-273.

Levidow, L., Carr, S., and Wield, D. (2000), 'Genetically modified crops in the European Union: regulatory conflicts as precautionary opportunities', *Journal of Risk Research*, 3 (3) pp. 189-208.

Limoges, C. (1993), 'Expert knowledge and decision-making in controversy contexts', *Public understanding of science*, 2, pp. 417-426.

Lindbladh, E. and Lyttkens, C.H. (2002), 'Habit versus choice: the process of decision-making in health-related behaviour', *Social Science and Medicine*, 55, pp. 451-465.

Marris, C., Wynne, B., Simmons, P. and Weldon, S. (2001), *Public Perceptions of Agricultural Biotechnologies in Europe*, Final report of the PABE research project. European Commission, available at www.pabe.net, accessed on 8/07/02

Martin, E. (1994), *Flexible bodies. Tracking immunity in American culture – from the days of polio to the age of AIDS*, Boston: Beacon Press.

McGuire, C. (1998), *Health Update: Immunisation*, London: Health Education Authority.

Mills, M. (1993), *Prevention, Health and British Politics*, Aldershot: Avery.

Mills, M. and Saward, M. (1993), 'Liberalism, democracy and prevention', in M. Mills *Prevention, Health and British Politics*, Aldershot: Avery.

Misztal, B.A. (1996), *Trust in Modern Societies: The Search for the Bases of Social Order*, Cambridge: Polity Press.

MORI (2002), 'Public's trust in doctors rises', available at www.mori.com/polls/2002/bma.shtml, accessed on 29/07/02.

Nasir, L. (2000), 'Reconnoitering the antivaccination web sites: news from the front', *Journal of Family Practice*, 49, 8, pp. 731-733, available at www.jfponline.com/content/2000/08/jfp_0800_07310.asp Accessed on 1/11/01.

Nettleton, S. (1997) 'Governing the risky self. How to become healthy, wealthy and wise', in A. Peterson and R. Bunton (eds), *Foucault, Health and Medicine*, London: Routledge.

NHS website (2002), *When Should You Vaccinate Your Child?*, Department of Health available at http://www.immunisation.org.uk/whento.html, accessed on 28/7/02.

NHS (2000), *The NHS Plan. A Plan For Investment. A Plan For Reform*, available at http://www.nhs.uk/nationalplan/, accessed on 29/07/02.

Petersen, A. (1997), 'Risk, governance and the new public health', in A. Petersen and R. Bunton. (eds), *Foucault, Health and Medicine*, London: Routledge.

Petersen, A. and Lupton, D. (1996), *The New Public Health. Health and Self in the Age of Risk*, London: Sage.

Phillips, A. (1999), *Dispelling Vaccination Myths. An Introduction To The Contradictions Between Medical Science and Immunization Policy*, York: Prometheus.

Poland, G.A and Jacobson, R.M. (2001), 'Understanding those who do not understand: a brief review of the anti-vaccine movement', *Vaccine*, 19, pp. 2440-2445.

Porter, D. and Porter, R. (1988), 'The politics of prevention: anti-vaccinationism and public health in nineteenth-century England', *Medical History*, 32, pp. 321-252.

Purdy, M. and Banks, D. (eds) (2001), *The Sociology and Politics of Health: A Reader*, London: Routledge.

Rogers, A. and Pilgrim, D. (1995), 'The risk of resistance: perspectives in the mass childhood immunisation (MCI) programme', in J.Gabe (ed.), *Medicine, Health and Risk: Sociological Approaches*, London: Blackwell.

Rogers, A. and Pilgrim, D. (1994), 'Rational non-compliance with childhood immunisation: personal accounts of parents and primary health care professionals', *Uptake of Immunisation. Issues for Health Educators*, London: Health Education Authority.

Rutgers, M.R. and Mentzel, M.A. (1999), 'Scientific expertise and public policy: resolving paradoxes?', in *Science and Public Policy*, 26 (3) pp. 146-150.

Sachs, L. (1996), 'Causality, responsibility and blame – core issues in the cultural construction and subtext of prevention', *Sociology of Health and Illness*, 18 (5) pp. 632-652.

Saks. M. (1994), 'Alternatives to medicine', in *Challenging Medicine*, J. Gabe., D. Kelleher, and G. Williams (eds), London: Routledge.

Scanlon, T.J. (2002), 'MMR vaccine may be lower than reported because of manipulation of target groups', *BMJ*, 324, p. 733.

Scott, A. (1990), *Ideology and the New Social Movements*, London: Unwin Hyman.

Shaw, I. (2002), 'How lay are lay beliefs?', *Health: An Interdisciplinary Journal for the Social Study of Health, Illness and Medicine*, 6 (3) pp. 287-299.

Spier, R.E. (2002), 'On the 2002 measles vaccination furore in the UK', *Vaccine*, 20, pp. 2845-2847.

Spier, R.E. (2001), 'Perceptions of risk of vaccines and adverse events: a historical perspective', *Vaccine*, 20, Supplement 1, pp. S78-S84.

Spier, R.E. (1998), 'Ethical aspects of vaccine and vaccination', *Vaccine*, 16 (19) pp. 1788-1794.

Streefland, P. H. (2001), 'Public doubts about vaccination safety and resistance against Vaccination', *Health Policy*, 55, pp. 159-172.

Taylor, M. (2002), 'An injection of doubt is required', The Informed Parent website, available at www.whale.to/vaccines/taylor.html, accessed on 27/07/02.

Thrower, D. (2001), 'MMR and late onset autism (Autistic Enterocolitis). A briefing note', Vaccine Awareness Network website, available at www.van.org.uk/mmr/index.html Accessed on 27/07/02.

van Eeten, M.J.G. (1999), 'Dialogues of the deaf' on science in policy controversies', *Science and Public Policy*, 26 (3) pp. 179-192.

Veermeersch, E. (1999), 'Individual rights versus societal duties', *Vaccine*, 17, pp. S14-S17.

Weingart, P. (1999), 'Scientific expertise and political accountability: paradoxes of science in politics', in *Science and Public Policy*, 26 (3) pp. 151-178.

What Doctors Don't Tell You (2002), 'About What Doctors Don't Tell You', available at www.wddty.co.uk/about.asp, accessed on 27/07/02.

Williams, S.J., Gabe, J., and Calnan, M. (eds) (2000), *Health, Medicine and Society. Key theories, future agendas*, London: Routledge.

Wood, B. (2000), 'Patient power?', *The Politics of Patient Associations in Britain and America*, Buckingham: Open University Press.

Wynne, B. (2001), 'Creating public alienation: Expert cultures of risk and ethics on GMOs', *Science as Culture*, 10 (4) pp. 445-481.

Wynne, B. (1993), 'Public uptake of science: a case for institutional reflexivity', *Public Understanding of Science*, 2, pp. 321-337.

Chapter 8

Pain, Loss and Collective Action: Health Consumer Groups and the Policy Process

Judith Allsop, Kathryn Jones and Rob Baggott

Introduction

In his presidential address to the 1998 American Political Science Association, Kent Jennings argued that human actions as a result of pain and loss experiences may move from individual to collective action. As a consequence, there is a shift from interaction in the private sphere to the sphere of the political (Jennings, 1999). He considers that the process through which this occurs should be studied more systematically by political scientists. The territory is also of interest to sociologists of health and illness. In this paper, the aim is to draw on data from a recently completed study of health consumer groups to explore, first, the link between pain and loss and group formation and, second, to identify the factors that may explain the more prominent role now being played by health consumer groups in the national level policy process.[1]

By 'pain and loss experiences' Jennings refers to those events associated with the body, within which illness, injury and death are major components. These events may be experienced directly, by someone with a medical condition, or indirectly, for example those with caring responsibility for sufferers or victims. They can be perceived as actually or potentially harmful or injurious, and responsibility and blame for such events can be attributed in various ways. They can be seen as having natural or supernatural causes: as due to biology, genetics, fate, 'acts of god' or as the consequence of human agency. In the latter case, events may be attributed to personal fault or to the acts of others. If others are involved, injurious events may be seen accidents or as wilful acts of hate, evil, revenge, incompetence or negligence. Depending on the social construction of attribution, people may decide simply to come to terms with these events, or they may take action that may bring them into the public sphere.

Jennings argues that there is an increased tendency for pain and loss experiences to reach the public sphere, and to result in collective action, because they are pervasive. Public opinion and the media can play a crucial role in turning a private sorrow into a public issue, and, thereafter, engagement with the political process. He calls for further study into the social and political construction such events and of who benefits and who loses from the politicisation of issues. This is a large agenda and beyond the scope of this chapter. However, in order to place the area within the sociological agenda, the next section will refer to indicative literature in the health and illness field and the remainder of the chapter will draw on the research on health consumer groups carried out by the authors.

From the Personal to the Political: A Selective Review

Within the sociology of health and illness in Britain, there are two areas of scholarship that have relevance to considering the shift from the personal to the political. First, the literature on what have been termed 'new social movements'; that is, those movements that have developed outside existing political structures and are characterised by a sense of shared identity related to a particular issue or status that is perceived as marginalised. Within the health and illness area some social movements, for example those concerning gender, sexuality, ethnicity or disability, have at least in part been associated with the body, pain and loss (see, Gabe, 1995). Certain social movements have had a profound effect in changing both the framework of assumptions and institutional forms either through radical action or through the formal political process or both. There are a number of important questions about how groups form, how they function and what factors affect their influence on the policy process which require more investigation.

In Britain, as far as empirical studies of group formation and political influence are concerned, some condition areas have been studied more than others. From the national policy perspective, the areas of disability (Campbell and Oliver, 1996); mental health (Rogers and Pilgrim, 1996) and to a lesser extent childbirth and maternity (Garcia et al., 1990) have attracted greater attention than cancer or chronic illness groups. However in the case of the latter two areas, there has been considerable work from the perspective of illness behaviour.

There have also been studies that have investigated group activity at the local level, such as Rogers and Pilgrim (1996) on mental health user groups; Weeks et al (1996) on HIV/AIDs voluntary groups; and Barnes et al. (1996) on the involvement of mental health user groups in service development and planning. Kelleher (1994) makes reference to why diabetes group form while a recent study by Small and Rhodes (2001) shows that there can be barriers to both group formation and to participation in group activity. An illness, particularly where this is progressive and debilitating, can be an insuperable barrier to social interaction.

Despite a long history of voluntary action in relation to pain and loss, until recently there have been few studies of the voluntary health sector as such. However, Hogg (1999) and Wood (2000) have begun to map the territory. Hogg looked at policies for patient involvement and the possibility for a patient's movement in Britain, and Wood examined a range of patients' groups in Britain and the United States. Both concluded that in terms of political influence, the patient's interest continued to be poorly articulated and relatively powerless within the context of British health policy when compared to professional, pharmaceutical and state/managerial interests.

The second area of scholarly research that has contributed to an understanding of the relationship between personal pain and loss and political action has been in the area of complaining in health care settings (Allsop, 1994; Nettleton and Harding, 1994; Mulcahy and Tritter, 1998; Allsop and Mulcahy 2001; Allsop et al., 2002). Nettleton and Harding (1994) saw complaining as a form of protest although they did not follow this through in terms of the political arena outside the institution studied. The other authors cited drew on attribution theory to suggest a causal link between the ways in which responsibility and blame for untoward events are attributed in health care settings to making, and persisting with, a complaint. The link between kinship networks and complaints was also identified. However, none of the studies looked at more collective forms of action, probably because these are relatively rare. Class action by sufferers has been the object of some investigation, for example in relation to thalidomide and also within the health and illness field in relation to tranquilliser use (Gabe and Bury, 1988).

While there may be a link between public opinion and the media and the success of collective action there is little understanding of what the transmission process is and why public opinion and the media support may be given to some causes rather than others. Schneider and Ingram (1987) suggest that both power and social approval may play a part in the social construction of a particular population. They do not analyse power but imply that traditional sources of influence, such as income and wealth, expertise, voting strength, numbers, and associations with institutionalised interests, can bring political leverage. In terms of social approval, a particular population may be seen as deserving/undeserving worthy of support or deviant and this too can influence the media and therefore the political process. While there are populations that are always seen as deserving, for example sick children, and those that tend to be seen as deviant, such as paedophilia groups or intra-venous drug users, others may be contenders in the social approval stakes.

Recently, Cole (2001) has commented that patient protest groups are growing in importance in Britain and may form quite quickly in response to a specific issue. For example, group formation followed in response to revelations about the storage of organs at the Alder Hey hospital and among parents whose children had been treated in a paediatric cardiology department in Bristol. The media coverage, the public inquiries (Royal Liverpool Children's Inquiry, 2001; Bristol Inquiry, 2001) contributed to a political response that went far beyond the concerns of the individuals themselves. This could be attributed to social approval for a cause, the power of a locality effect when cases are clustered in one area and a fit with the wider government policy agenda to increase professional regulation. In Britain with its centralised government structure, this may be a particularly significant factor. The next section of the chapter will focus on health consumer groups. It will draw on the research study which, in general terms, aimed to identify their characteristics, explore the relationship between groups, central government and other health care stakeholders in the light of recent governments' emphasis on a participation agenda. Data collection for the project took place in 1999/2000.

The Study of Health Consumer Groups: Scope and Methods

In the research, health consumer groups, were defined as voluntary sector organisations concerned with promoting and/or representing the interests of users and/or carers in the health arena at national level. A summary of the findings is available elsewhere (Jones et al., 2000; Baggott et al. 2001). In terms of the research design, there was an initial quantitative survey that 'mapped' the area. This was followed by the collection of qualitative data through interview so that similarities and differences between groups could be identified (Bryman, 1988: 137). In the absence of a suitable database, it was not possible to include every group so the aim was to produce a data set that consisted of as many groups as could be identified across five condition areas. These were arthritis, cancer, heart and circulatory disease, maternity and childbirth, and mental health, and were chosen to reflect a range of patient, user and carer experiences and different policy priorities. Generic consumer groups that focused on a particular population but had health in their remit such as Age Concern, the Carers National Association and Action for Sick Children, were also identified, as well as 'umbrella' or what we called formal alliance organisations. The latter were groups that were composed of a number of other autonomous groups, such as the Patients Forum, the Genetic Interest Group and the Long Term Medical Conditions Alliance.

A number of data sources were used to identify groups and subsequently, a number of boundary decisions had to be made. In stage one, a structured postal questionnaire with open-ended questions was developed to establish the characteristics and activities of groups and the extent of their interaction with government and other stakeholders. Organisations who returned a questionnaire but did not meet the entry criteria[2] were excluded. The final data set consisted of 186 groups. The effective response rate was 66 per cent (n=123). Semi-structured interviews were then undertaken with key informants from structured sample of 39 health consumer groups, followed by interviews with 31 members of political elites such as civil servants, MPs, the professional associations, research charities, the pharmaceutical sector and general consumer groups.

The interviews were analysed to develop a grounded theory of the internal relationships between the group leaders and their membership and external relations between groups and other health care stakeholders. The aim was also to compare different types of group and to assess the ways in which health consumer groups were involved in the policy process, why they were involved and to assess their contribution in the light of the opinion of a range of respondents. The method adopted, which was to interview group officials, both those who were elected and salaried officers, meant that our findings reflected the views of leaders rather than rank-and-file members. There is a gap in the literature as there is little research on who joins health sector groups, and who does not, as well as on the internal dynamics of groups from the members' perspective.

Pain and Loss: The Formation and Characteristics of Health Consumer Groups

The main common denominator of the survey data set was that the target population of health consumer groups were people who directly and indirectly, were affected by matters related to a particular aspect of the bodily functioning, illness or suffering. The broad aim of the vast majority of groups was to provide support and act as a pressure group for this actual or potential population who were, to some extent, disadvantaged by virtue of their status or condition. Once these broad generalisations have been made, there was considerable diversity although, as will be argued below, there are structural and political factors that pull groups towards collaboration despite this diversity.

In terms of formation, the health consumer groups in the data set had been established in different periods and drew on different traditions. The questionnaire data indicated that about 10 per cent of health consumer groups were formed before 1960; a quarter between 1961 and 1980 and two-thirds after 1981. The finding supports Wood's (2000: 36) claim that growth since 1980 has been rapid, although without a baseline from which to measure growth, this cannot be demonstrated quantitatively.

Some groups had been formed for altruistic and philanthropic reasons to support the under-privileged; some to pursue the social rights of vulnerable groups. Others were established to provide mutual support. In the case of a number of the more recently formed groups, the aim was to build a shared sense of identity through the common experience of a particular illness or condition. This was manifest in the varying degrees of emphasis on mutual support, campaigning to improve services and protest over particular aspects of government policy. Groups in the data set rarely engaged in more radical forms of protest.

In terms of the social construction, the trigger for the establishment of a number of recently formed condition groups has been an individual personal experience, followed by the identification of others in a similar position and group formation. For example, at least three cancer groups Cancer BACUP (1985) the National Cancer Alliance (1994) and Cancer Black Care (1995) were initiated by people with a personal or family experience of cancer. In the case of Cancer BACUP, the founder was also a doctor (Clement-Jones 1985). The Archnoiditis Trust (1987), a small arthritis-related group, developed from a chance meeting between two sufferers in an out-patient department and a concern about the poor quality of service. A number of other groups, such as SANDS (1981), which is a support group for parents who experience a stillbirth or neo-natal death, and TAMBA (1978) for parents with twins and multiple births,[3] have developed in the maternity and childbirth area. Clearly, organisational skills and social networks are necessary to find common cause with others. The media can play a role in this process. For example, the National Schizophrenia Fellowship (1972) was formed after a carer shared her experiences through the pages of *The Times*. Wide media coverage played a part in assisting the formation of the Zito Trust, which was established by Jane Zito following the death of her husband.

Some groups have been formed on the initiative of, or with support from, the medical profession. This was most likely with groups in the arthritis and heart and circulatory disease areas, such as the National Ankylosing Spondylitis Society (1976) founded with support from rheumatologists, and the British Cardiac Patients Association (1982), formed at the suggestion of heart specialists at the Harefield Hospital.

In an earlier decade, a number of groups were established as offshoots of an existing charity that had recognised a particular unmet 'need'. These are typically groups that try to facilitate particular forms of development. For example, Help the Aged (1961) was established at the instigation of Oxfam. The College of Health (1983) had its origins in the Consumers' Association. This tradition still persists with, for example, the Afyia Trust (1996), an organisation set up by the Kings Fund (London) to support black and ethnic minority community networks especially in relation to mental health but now with a wider remit.

The impetus for formal alliance organisations, those made up of other autonomous groups, has generally come from key individuals within the voluntary health sector who perceived benefits in greater co-ordination of effort and the need to support smaller groups. Such groups are of relatively recent foundation and reflect a concern to build a consensus and contribute effectively to policy development.

Organisations in the voluntary sector have been notoriously difficult to classify and the health sector is no exception. As Kendall and Knapp (1996) have pointed out, there are fuzzy boundaries between types of organisations and the roles that people play. For example, a distinction has been made between those voluntary health sector groups that act *for* sufferers and those that are composed *of* sufferers.

This distinction is difficult to sustain in the light of evidence from the field. Although most of the groups in the data set were membership groups (92 per cent), a few of these were run by an elite. Among the remaining 8 per cent, were some charities of long standing that provided services under contract. These were committed to the principle and practice of user involvement. In either case, there were a variety of ways in which the client group was included in decision making. For example, some groups employed the client group in project work, appointed representatives to their governing body or canvassed their client group for their views on policy proposals.

Overall, there has been a trend over time towards more groups being formed by sufferers themselves. However, even if a group has been established by sufferers, there is a trend towards employing paid officials to carry out management and administrative tasks. The data indicated that these people have themselves often been 'sufferers', either directly or indirectly, and that personal experience can lead them to seek employment in the sector. Organisations that play a facilitative or co-ordinating role have also been on the increase. These factors may have contributed to a shift towards more participative structures as groups seek to gain credibility and acceptance in the political sphere.

Health consumer groups are extremely diverse. They differ in their focus, size, structure, financial and human resources, longevity, history and traditions. To take two examples: in terms of income, 16 per cent of health consumer groups had an annual income of less that £10,000 per annum while 6 per cent had an income of over £10 million. Although most groups had a membership, this varied between the 15 per cent that had a hundred members or less to the 6 per cent with more than ten thousand members.

Groups were structured in different ways; for example, about half of the groups had a devolved branch structure, so although the national body might be run by paid staff, the local branches were not. Some were run directly from a national headquarters. This varied from those with a London-based headquarters with a prestigious address to groups operating from a founder's front-room in the provincial suburbs.

However, almost all groups carried out a range of activities that covered both providing a service to influencing policy. The former typically included providing information for their members/clients and the public; raising awareness of an illness or condition, and giving advice or facilitating support networks for the public in contact. Groups also undertook organisation maintenance activities such as fundraising, informing and consulting with members or client groups, as well as networking and seeking to influence national policy through campaigning and lobbying. Furthermore, between two-thirds and three-quarters of groups said they provided education and training and promoted research. Over half said they aimed to influence the provision of local services.

The Political Context of Health Consumer Groups

Some reference has been made to the social construction of health consumer groups in terms of formation. A further aspect of this social construction is the political context in which groups operate. In analysing the interview data it was apparent that, despite their diversity, health consumer group leaders operated within a shared 'assumptive world'. They operated within a common set of national institutional and referred to a similar norms and values. It will be argued that these factors may explain the increasingly collaborative relationships and structures that have drawn health consumer groups towards what they have in common rather than their differences. In addition, the health policies pursued by Labour governments since 1997 have created further incentives for alliances and collaboration. However, these vary between condition areas in ways that are again shaped by the political context.

A shared Institutional framework

In Britain, there is a tax-incentive to obtaining registration as a charity. Most groups (91 per cent) in the questionnaire data set were registered as charities. They were therefore subject to the same set of rules and regulations that govern charitable status and which are administered through the Charity Commission. This status brings an element of accountability and a requirement not to engage in overtly party-political activity. The few groups that were *not* registered were either very small or put a high value on independence and had sufficient funding to go it alone.

A further common factor was that, without exception, groups in the data set were concerned to improve the quality of services within the National Health Service. Those interviewed had a commitment to public provision and to values associated with this such as a concern for equality of access and common standards, irrespective of geographical location. There was therefore a shared interest in working within NHS policy networks and keeping up-to-date with policy changes. Virtually no mention was made by interviewees of the private sector.[4] The broad agenda addressed by most health consumer groups is reflected in the following comment:

> (it) isn't just a political agenda but it's actually a whole NHS and Social Services agenda...... a significant proportion is actually working within the NHS and we also have our managers [who] are focusing very much on working with local NHS trusts and PCGs and PCTs in trying to improve the services in their local areas, so it's a two-pronged attack (Condition Based Group).

As well as a commitment to the NHS, analysis of the interviews showed that health consumer groups shared other core values. There was a belief in the existence of, and the value of, 'lay knowledge'; in the importance of participatory processes; a commitment to the inclusion of disadvantaged groups and, in terms of process, a commitment to networking in order to influence policy outcomes.

The value of experiential knowledge

Most groups referred to the importance of the experiential knowledge that came from living with, or caring for someone with, a particular illness or condition. The importance of lay knowledge in shaping social constructions and affecting responses to health policy has received some attention in the health and illness literature (for example, see Stacey, 1994). Kelleher (1998) draws on Habermas' (1984) notion of the 'lifeworld of ordinary people' to explain the kind of experience gained by people who live with diabetes. This type of knowledge is contrasted with the expert knowledge of bio-medicine and the 'instrumental rationality' that focuses on the goal of diagnosing and treating disease and rests on particular concepts and theories of an abstract formal system. Such knowledge tends to isolate the sufferer and may inhibit the process of coming to terms with the afflictions of the body.

In discussing the types of knowledge held by organisations, Lam (2000) refers to 'embodied knowledge'. This is individual, tacit, action-oriented, practical and context specific knowledge. She also refers to 'embrained knowledge' that rests on particular cognitive schema; 'encoded knowledge' that is collective and explicit and 'embedded knowledge' that is collectively shared but based on shared norms and routines.

The analysis of the interviews indicated that as organisations, health consumer group leaders set great store on the embodied, experiential knowledge of those who lived with, either directly or vicariously, with a disease or condition. This was used internally as a social resource within the organisation to provide support. For example, one respondent said:

> They [members who have experienced a condition] can empathise far more deeply ... Their level of knowledge never ceases to amaze me (Formal Alliance Organization).

Another aspect of this lay knowledge was the experience of sufferers or carers in using NHS services. Frequently, data were collected to make that knowledge more explicit and codified. For example, most health consumer groups (80 per cent) in the questionnaire data set had telephone helplines for both members and the general public. Interview data showed that calls to these helplines were analysed in order to identify problems and trends. These data were used as a resource when engaging in political activity. Many groups (48 per cent) said they undertook research on particular issues such as age discrimination within the National Health Service, or on the treatment options being offered to people with schizophrenia.

Health consumer groups also drew on the knowledge of bio-medicine. As one respondent said:

> I didn't know anything about medical matters before. I reckon I could pass an exam now to be a doctor. You tend to self-educate yourself that much (Condition Based Group).

Lay membership networks were an important conduit for channelling information through the organisation. Bio-medical knowledge was also accessed through professional members or associates, from databases on evidence-based practice or the internet and circulated within the group. The questionnaire data showed that almost three-quarters (71 per cent) of condition-based groups had professionals in their membership. These were, in the main, doctors.

The value of participatory and inclusive practices

On the basis of their collective knowledge of the lay experience, health consumer group leaders developed a view of their policy priorities. Almost all interviewees placed a high value on participatory processes to involve their membership in policy formation. Embodied and embedded knowledge was developed through interaction between members and between members and headquarters using a variety of means of communication, such as the telephone, websites, meetings, seminars, conferences and regular newsletters and member surveys. Helplines and face-to-face support were typically run through member networks. These informal networks were a social resource for health consumer groups. Except for very small groups, formal channels for election to a decision-making body existed alongside informal ways for involving rank and file members.

Most health consumer groups were sensitive to external audiences within government and with other health care stakeholders. By seeking to ground their claims to be heard in lay experience and participatory practices, health consumer groups aimed to enhance their credibility and to gain social approval. Groups were aware that in terms of the usual sources of institutionalised power - money, monopoly position or electoral position - they were relatively weak. For example, almost all groups referred to a shortage of funding in relation to their aims and objectives. Small groups in terms of resources or membership believed they were disadvantaged in relation to the larger charities. In addition, groups in all condition areas mentioned problems in retaining an active and continuous membership due to the temporary nature of the condition (as in pregnancy); periodic serious illness or disability (as in mental health and arthritis); terminal illness (as with some cancer and heart groups). As Small and Rhodes (2000) found, serious illness can be a barrier to joining a group as well as participating actively.

A number of groups referred to their difficulties in attracting ethnic minority members and saw this as a weakness, especially in terms of attracting government funding. Some groups had made efforts to provide information materials in a range of languages - through setting up special advisory groups, commissioning research or appointing representatives from particular groups to their governing board. A small number of national health consumer groups specifically represent ethnic minorities.

Groups were also sensitive to public opinion. Some groups referred to not being a 'popular' cause. This could be because the condition itself was stigmatising, unfashionable or affected only a very small group in the population. The cause could be seen as a 'middle class' issue or, as in the case of care in the community for those with a mental illness, there was seen to be a conflict between the concern of many groups for civil rights and issues of public safety that were promoted in the popular press. Most health consumer groups acknowledged the importance of the media's portrayal of health issues and had frequent contact with the media. In the questionnaire, three-quarters of the respondents said they regarded links with the media important and just under half reported monthly contact. In interview, groups referred to a wide range of media contacts with the press, radio and television. Contacts were both proactive and responsive. The larger organisations often employed specialist staff to deal with the media. Groups used the media to raise awareness, publicise campaigns and put pressure on government to address what they considered to be poor practice or a failing service. From the data, elderly people and cancer sufferers, particularly when they can be linked to failings in the National Health Service, both attracted favourable media coverage (see Seale, 2001). Yet other groups, particularly in the arthritis area, said the media was disinterested in their cause. Even those groups that received generally favourable coverage, believed that the popular media could over-simplify and sensationalise issues by reinforcing particular stereotypes or highlighting untypical cases.

Alliances and Networking

In recent years, a major structural change in the voluntary health sector has been the formation of a number of formal alliance or 'umbrella' groups. By seeking to identify a common interest and link together autonomous groups, formal alliances have a clear political aim – to increase influence on policy. Each condition area within the research contained some form of formal alliance group, albeit each with a different role. For example, the Maternity Alliance is a broadly-based pressure group that includes trade unions and is concerned with issues related to the health, welfare and employment that arise with maternity. The British League for Arthritis and Rheumatism includes professional associations as well as patient and carer groups. Within the mental health field, the UK Federation of Smaller Mental Health Agencies has been established to support the smaller groups.

There are also sector-wide groups such as the Patients Forum, which includes professional as well as patient and carer groups. Established in 1990, and now with nearly 70 members, it provides a forum for updating, networking and information exchange. The Long Term Medical Conditions Alliance (LMCA) was founded in 1989 and by 2002 had well over a hundred other organisations as members. Although it initially focused on long term conditions, it now includes a wider range of groups. The LMCA, as well as providing support and information has aimed to develop the managerial capacity of smaller groups.

As Hojnacki (1998), in her analysis of alliances between groups in Washington politics, argues, organisations face choices about the extent of collaboration. According to a 'rational actor' model of the policy process, this will be based on a calculation of the benefits and costs for each organisation. Based on an analysis of the groups in the data set, while interviewees acknowledged that they were in competition with each other for members, public attention and funding, they nevertheless joined alliances or coalitions when these were seen to bring benefits. These benefits were seen to be in terms of developing capacity, sharing workloads, pooling knowledge and expertise and influencing policy. Questionnaire data showed that almost nine out of ten groups claimed that their organisation had links or alliances with other user/carer organisations, and three quarters viewed this as a key facilitator in the policy process.

As well as formal alliances, a number of looser coalitions and networks provided a way of sharing information and co-ordinating activities. These sometimes included professional associations. However, there were differences in the way that alliances were constructed within different condition areas. Strategic informal coalitions were particularly well developed between maternity and mental health groups reflecting perhaps the greater longevity of groups in these sectors, their shared de-medicalisation agenda and their previous experience of working together. For example, maternity and childbirth groups worked together in the early 1990s on the 'changing childbirth' agenda (Expert Maternity Group, 1993).

More recently, informal alliances have developed in these sectors between health consumer groups and the medical profession. In the late 1990s, the Mental Health Alliance was formed, a loose association of about 40 groups, including the Royal College of GPs. Opposition to the Labour Government's proposals to amend the 1983 Mental Health Act has brought closer collaboration between the Royal College of Psychiatrists and the Mental Health Alliance. Maternity and childbirth groups and professional associations from both medicine and midwifery have also found a common interest in raising the profile of the maternity services through establishing an All Party Parliamentary Group on maternity services and responding to the high rates of caesarean section in Britain (Boseley, 2001; RCOG, RCM and NCT, 2002).

The Policy Environment and Health Consumer Groups

As well as increased confidence in a knowledge base in 'lay experience', a greater structuring within the sector, shifts in government policy have also promoted the involvement of health consumer groups in the policy process. First, the voluntary sector has been supported. For Conservative governments this was in the interest of developing a mixed economy of welfare. Labour governments, have placed more emphasis on the role of the voluntary sector in civil society (Kendall and Knapp, 1999; Home Office, 1998; Passey et al., 2000; NCVO/CCS, 2001).

Second, within the Department of Health, Ministers have often taken a lead in encouraging consultation with health consumer groups and, in 1996, the then NHS Executive (1996) promoted change within the Department itself through a strategy to 'practice what we preach' – in other words, if user consultation is being promoted at local level, civil servants should follow suit. This message appears to have borne fruit. The questionnaire data showed that three quarters of health consumer groups had been in contact with central government on policy issues within the previous three years and almost two thirds believed that opportunities for participation had increased. Formal alliance organisations were in most frequent contact with government.

Financial support from government has been forthcoming, albeit at a modest level. For example, in 1998/9, the Department of Health supported the voluntary health and social care sector through core and project grants worth around £20.8 million. About one third of the health consumer groups in the research data set had received central government funding – mainly for special projects of short duration.

Third, a number of institutions established by Labour governments since 1997 have included lay representatives often drawn from health consumer groups, as they are considered to have expertise, represent a wider constituency and have managerial capacity. The National Institute for Clinical Excellence (NICE) has a Partners' Council composed of health consumer groups, professionals and representatives of the drugs industry. In interview, several respondents mentioned involvement with NICE. Groups had submitted evidence and some had been represented on appraisal groups and on the Partners' Council. While a few interviewees saw involvement as tokenistic, others believed that there were opportunities to enhance their role (see also Quennell, 2001; Duckenfield, 2002). The Commission for Health Improvement, which now has additional powers as a health inspectorate, appoints review and investigative teams with lay as well as professional members. It also consults with patients and local groups.

The working parties established to develop national service frameworks for health service priorities and to implement the NHS Plan (DOH, 2000) have all contained representatives from health consumer groups (Hogg, 2002). Most recently, under the National Health Service Reform and Health Professions Act 2002, a national Commission for Patient and Public Involvement in Health will provide leadership for new local level bodies.

Both political and practical considerations may explain the more extensive engagement with health consumer groups. In terms of membership, the voluntary health sector as a whole covers a substantial constituency. Many groups have local branches. The larger groups and alliances can devote resources both to contribute to, and influence, the political process. As far as governments are concerned, the existence of a health consumer lobby may be welcome in curbing other corporate interests such as medicine and the pharmaceutical industry. (Mort et al., 1996). It can also be argued that health consumer groups can contribute to policy formation in a creative way by drawing on the experiential knowledge of their constituency. For example, the LMCA developed the concept of self management in chronic illness and worked with government to develop the 'Expert Patient' programme (Department of Health, 2001). According to a number of interviewees, the Patients Forum played an important role in coordinating a response and securing amendments to the 1999 Health Bill. Both the Patient's Forum and an Advisory Group consisting of health consumer groups, general consumer groups and representatives from community health councils contributed to proposals for a Commission on Patient and Public Involvement (Allsop et al., 2002).[5]

Within the voluntary health sector, particular health consumer groups and certain condition areas were, according to those interviewed, seen as 'insiders' in the policy process. Insiders were the larger alliance groups, the larger London-based condition groups and a wider range of condition groups where there was a fit with government priorities. For example, interviewees from both the medical and nursing professions saw the cancer groups, and particularly those associated with breast cancer as having had a major influence on policy. Although prostate cancer has about the same incidence as breast cancer, prostate cancer support groups had a lower profile.

Although the participation of health consumer groups has increased, it could be argued that agendas are still controlled by others. When health consumer groups collaborate with government or with the medical profession or the pharmaceutical industry, it is the latter groups who determine the agenda. Consumer groups have few, if any, sanctions to apply. Nevertheless, health care politics have become more open to a range of influences as medical hegemony has declined and the pharmaceutical industry is subject to greater controls at least within Britain. Health consumer groups, particularly those that have special expertise, or can offer practical and workable solutions, have become insiders in the policy process. This presents both dangers and opportunities. The danger is that leaders of insider groups will become divorced from their membership. The opportunity is for the interests of health care consumers will be represented effectively in the policy process.

Conclusion

In this chapter, it has been suggested that sociologists of health and illness have much to contribute to investigating the processes through which personal experiences of pain and loss can trigger group formation and collective action. Both the literature on social movements and the analysis of complaining behaviour provides a foundation, but there should be further investigation of particular groups and the circumstances of their formation.

From the research on health consumer groups, the target populations of which have had direct or indirect experience of pain and loss, it was found that a number of groups had recently been by people who had direct experience of a condition or illness either directly or vicariously. Both the media and the health professions could play a role. However, other groups that had been formed in an earlier period have also sought to involve their target population in their decision-making and activities.

The involvement and influence of health consumer groups in the national policy process has been growing. It has been argued that this is due to a number of factors. Health consumer groups base their claims to be heard on experiential, embodied knowledge. They aim to engage their membership/clients in participatory practices. They are committed to improving the quality of the National Health Service. Structural changes in the sector have occurred through the formation of alliance groups. These enhance the claims to represent a broad constituency.

At the same time, the political context has changed. For government and other stakeholders there are now seen to be political advantages in engagement with health consumer groups. Opportunities for engagement have increased and health consumer groups and particularly those seen to offer solutions or which are politically and socially approved are being incorporated into the policy process. Theoretically, this can be seen as a 'paradigm shift' within the health arena in interest group representation, as described by Baumgartner and Jones (1993). This offers a number of interesting new areas for further investigation.

Notes

1   ESRC Grant Number R000237888.
2   Given the focus on user/carer interests, research charities and professional associations were not considered to be consumer organizations although they were interviewed as stakeholders. Also excluded were general consumer organizations, as health was only part of their brief, disability organizations, as they had already been extensively researched, local/regional groups and statutory organisations such as CHCs and organizations that provided helplines only.

3   SANDS – Stillbirth and Neonatal Death Society, TAMBA – Twins and Multiple Births Association.
4   There are groups that relate specifically to the private sector. For other groups, NHS issues were presumably dominant.
5   Through the Patients Forum website. The proposals were enacted through the NHS and Health Professions Act 2002.

References

Allsop, J. (1994), 'Two sides to every story: the perspectives of complainants and doctors', *Law and Policy*, 16 (2), 148-83.

Allsop, J. and Mulcahy, L. (2001), 'Dealing with clinical complaints', in C. Vincent (ed.) *Clinical Risk Management: Enhancing Patient Safety*, 2nd Edition, London: BMA Books.

Allsop, J., Baggott, R. and Jones, K. (2002), 'Hearing Voices', *Health Service Journal*, 28 March, 28-29.

Baggott, R., Allsop J. and Jones, K. (2001), *Health Consumer Groups and the National Policy Process*, End of Award Report to the Economic and Social Research Council.

Barnes, M., Harrison, S., Mort, M.; Shardlow, P. and Wistow, G. (1996), 'Users, officials and citizens in health and social care', *Local Government Policy Making*, 22(4), 8-17.

Baumgartner, F. and Jones, B. (1993), *Agendas and Instability in American Politics*, Chicago: University of Chicago Press.

Boseley, S. (2001), 'Caesarean births soar to one in five', *The Guardian*, 26 November, 13.

Bristol Inquiry (2001), *Learning from Bristol*, Public Inquiry into Children's Heart Surgery at the Bristol Royal Infirmary 1984-1995, London: The Stationery Office.

Bryman, A. (1988), *Social Research Methods*, Oxford: Oxford University Press.

Campbell, J. and Oliver, M. (1996), *Disability Politics*, London: Routledge.

Clement-Jones, V. (1985), Cancer and beyond: the formation of BACUP, *British Medical Journal*, 291, 6501.

Cole, P. (2001), 'Movers and Shakers', *Health Service Journal*, 30 August, 23-7.

DOH (2000), *The NHS Plan: A Plan for Investment, a Plan for Reform*, Cm 4818-1, London: The Stationery Office.

Department of Health (2001), *The Expert Patient: a New Approach to Chronic Disease Management for the 21st Century*, London: Department of Health.

Duckenfield, M. (2002), *'Patient Power?: Patient Groups Influence in the Drug Approval Process in the UK'*, Paper presented at the 2002 Annual Meeting of the Political Studies Association, Aberdeen, 5-7 April.

Expert Maternity Group (1993) *Changing Childbirth Part 1: Report of the Expert Maternity Group*, London: HMSO.

Gabe, J. (ed.) (1995), *Medicine, Health and Risk: Sociological Approaches*, Sociology of Health and Illness Monograph Series, Oxford: Blackwell.

Gabe, J. and Bury, M. (1988), 'Tranquillisers as a social problem', *Sociological Review*, 36 (2), 320-352.

Garcia, J., Patrick, R. and Richards, M. (1990), *The Politics of Maternity Care: Services for Childbearing Women in 20th Century Britain*, Oxford: Oxford University Press.

Habermas, J. (1984), *The Theory of Communicative Action Volume 1. Reason and the Rationalisation of Society*, Boston Mass: Beacon Press.

Hogg, C. (1999), *Patients and Power: Health Policy from a User Perspective*, London: Sage.

Hogg, C. (2002), *National Service Frameworks: Involving Patients and the Public*, London: Patients Forum.

Hojnacki, M. (1998), 'Interest groups' decisions to join alliances or work alone', *American Journal of Political Science*, 41, 61-87.

Home Office (1998), *Compact Getting in Right Together: Compact on Relations Between Government and the Voluntary and Community Sector in England*, Cm 4100 London: Home Office.

Jennings, K. (1999), 'Political responses to pain and loss: presidential address 1998 American Political Science Association', *American Political Science Review*, 93(1), 1-15.

Jones, K., Baggott, R. and Allsop, J. (2000), 'Under the influence?', *Health Service Journal*, 16 November, 28-29.

Kelleher, D. (1994), 'Self-help groups and their relationship to medicine', in J Gabe, D.Kelleher and G.Williams (eds), *Challenging Medicine*, London: Routledge

Kendall, J. and Knapp, J. (1996), *The Voluntary Sector in the UK*, Manchester: Manchester University Press.

Lam, A. (2000), 'Tacit knowledge, organisational learning and societal institutions – an integrated framework', *Organisational Studies*, 21, 487-513.

Mort M., Harrison, S. and Wistow, G. (1996), 'The user card: breaking through the organisational undergrowth in health and social care', *Contemporary Political Studies*, 2, 1133-1140.

Mulcahy, L. and Tritter, J. (1998), 'Pathways, pyramids and icebergs? Mapping the links between dissatisfaction and complaints', *Sociology of Health and Illness*, 20(6), 825-847.

NCVO/CCS (2001), *Next Steps in Voluntary Action*, London: National Council for Voluntary Organisations/Centre for Civil Society.

Nettleton, S. and Harding, G. (1994), 'Protesting patients: A study of complaints submitted to a Family Health Service Authority', *Sociology of Health and Illness*, 2(1), 38-61.

NHS Executive (1996), *Patient Partnership Building a Collaborative Strategy*, Leeds: Department of Health.

Passey, A., Hems, L. and Jas, P. (2000), *The UK Sector Almanac*, London: National Council for Voluntary Organizations.

Rogers, A. and Pilgrim, D. (1996), *Mental Health Policy in Britain*, London: Macmillan.

RCOG; RCM; NCT (2002), 'The rising caesarean rate – from audit to action', Report of a joint conference organized by the Royal College of Obstetricians and Gynaecologists, the Royal College of Midwives and the National Childbirth Trust, London: National Childbirth Trust.

Royal Liverpool Children's Inquiry (2001), *Summary and Recommendations*, London: House of Commons.

Quennell, P. (2001), 'Getting their say, or getting their way?', *Journal of Management in Medicine*, 15(3), 201-219.

Schneider, A. and Ingram, H. (1987), 'The social construction of target populations: implications for politics and policy', *American Political Science Review*, 1(2), 334-347

Seale, C. (2001), 'Sporting cancer: struggle language in news reports of people with cancer', *Sociology of Health and Illness*, 23(3), 308-329.

Small, N. and Rhodes, P. (2000), *Too Ill to Talk? User Involvement in Palliative Care*, London: Routledge.

Stacey, M. (1994), 'The power of lay knowledge', in J. Popay and G. Williams (eds) *Researching the People's Health*, London: Routledge.

Tyler, S. (2002), 'Comparing the campaigning profile of maternity user groups in Europe - can we learn anything useful?, *Health Expectations*, 5(2), 136-147.

Weeks, J., Aggleton, P., McKevitt, C., Parkinson, K. and Taylor-Labourn, A. (1996), 'Community and contracts: tensions and dilemmas in the voluntary sector response to HIV and AIDS', *Policy Studies*, 17(2), 107-123.

Wood, B. (2000), *Patient Power? The Politics of Patients Associations in Britain and America*, Buckinghamshire: Open University Press.

Chapter 9

The Medicalisation of Unhappiness?
The Management of Mental Distress
in Primary Care

Ian Shaw and Louise Woodward

Introduction

The concept of medicalisation has received increasing attention over the past three decades (Conrad, 2000). Whilst earlier work tended to focus upon the medicalisation of deviance (Pitts, 1968) this soon extended to the application of the concept to a wide range of human behaviours. Over the years a vast literature has developed on the medicalisation of such problems, with particularly attention given to the medical domain (Friedson, 1970; Zola, 1972; Illich, 1975; Conrad, 2000). As more traditional advocates (Illich, 1975) of the concept lay claims to the illegitimate power and influence health professionals display over patients, in more recent years this concept has been extended to give consideration to the medicalisation of daily living. Thus, high rates of medicalisation may be indicative of systemic problems in Western Society and consequently the notion of the population itself medicalising problems is an increasingly important aspect to the debate. The issue addressed within this paper is the extent to which the public is driving medicalisation and the extent to which it may be a result of doctors.

A Brief Summary of the Medicalisation Thesis

The medicalisation thesis has a number of varied definitions. In its basic form, it could be defined as the power exerted by the medical profession, in primarily serving themselves rather than their patients (Friedson, 1988). Advocates of this critique lay claim to doctors attempting to enhance their position by presenting themselves as possessing the exclusive right to define and treat illness (Peterson and Bunton, 1997: 96). A more basic interpretation sees medicalisation as the illegitimate extension of the power and influence of medicine. 'Illegitimate' for a number of reasons; first of all, by making more claims upon medical achievements than can be scientifically justified. Furthermore, psychiatry has been regarded by some as having a pre-occupation with social behaviour and controlling that behaviour that is labelled as 'bad' (Szasz, 1970; Rosen, 1972). As far back as the early part of the twentieth century public health was high on the government's agenda. Post Second World War Britain witnessed a Mental Hygiene Movement, with its focus upon reducing those social ills caused by mental disturbance (Rose, in Miller and Rose, 1986). This was sought through the promotion of mental welfare and mental hygiene and it was here that the rationale for a new 'social psychiatry' developed, which located the cause of many ills in society as a direct result of an individual's mental health. Such behaviour was to be controlled or, if possible, prevented by 'education, early detection of signs of trouble and prompt and efficient treatment' (Rose, in Miller and Rose, 1986:49). This preoccupation with control and managing social behaviour has led the medical profession, in some cases, to make scientific claims upon, sometimes, minimal evidence, which stand as medical advancements.

A second point concerns medicalisation as an illegitimate extension of professional power. Whilst this concept tends towards more traditional theories within the medicalisation debate, of the abuse of professional power in relation to the patient's position, it nevertheless remains an important one. Illich (1975) suggests that people's health is undermined by today's medicine through judging lay people's inability to determine their own healthcare. At the heart of the medicalisation critique is this idea that individuals should be constrained by the medical profession (Petersen and Bunton 1997). Relationships, which exist between doctors and patients, are but one clear illustration of this power imbalance and autonomy exerted within medicine. The traditional argument lays claim to the limited medical knowledge lay people display places them in a vulnerable bargaining position with their GPs, and increases the powerlessness of the sick person (Fox, 1997). Consequently this can lead to an over reliance upon the professional diagnosis. Petersen and Bunton (1997: 96) assert that 'research undertaken on the doctor-patient relationship have focused on ways the medical consultation facilitates power of doctors over patients and supports capitalist ideologies'.

Thirdly, medicine can be seen as illegitimate in deflecting cultural challenges to the existing social and cultural order by transferring these challenges into individual problems rather than viewing them as collectively or structurally caused. Concerns are raised over social problems becoming de-contextualised by the medical model and, consequently, where biographical solutions are sought for systemic contradictions (Bauman, 2001). As Eaton (2001: 28) suggests 'the system has expanded to define a wider and wider range of behaviours as medical illness'. The word 'behaviour' in itself rather than 'condition' for example, denotes it is of individual making rather than a social or economic construction. Thus, shifting the focus of the problem away from the social and towards the individual.

Some advocates of the medicalisation critique (Zola, 1999) suggest that virtually all of our day-to-day activities have been illustrated by medical representations of what is normal (health) and what is abnormal (ill health), suggesting that our entire existence is becoming medicalised. With the post First World War mental hygiene movement, even mild mental disturbances were given psychiatric attention. These were deemed to cause social inefficiency and personal unhappiness (Rose, in Miller and Rose, 1986). Nowadays, public tolerance for unhappiness has decreased with the emerging medicalisation of human distress. Perhaps the increasing medicalisation of deviant behaviour and social control can be seen in the way depression has become prevalent in the past decade. (The apparatus of treatments and social control, with particular reference to anti-depressants, has increased in the last decade, with 17.5 million Benzodiazapine prescriptions issued by GPs in 1999) (Panorama, BBC 1, 13/05/01). One possible explanation for this is rooted in the alienating effects of a changing individualistic and competitive world. It has been argued that alienation within contemporary society is increasing and has become manifest in the medicalisation of social problems; 'New forms of illness are being called into being, and boundaries of existing illness definitions extended within biomedicine and culture at large' (Lyon, 1996: 57). The argument follows that during a climate of social alienation the 'context of the self is important, as it becomes an object of intervention'. The social, cultural, economic and emotional context of the individual are all important and it is this context which illustrates how depression has become positioned within contemporary medicine (Lyon, 1996) and, consequently, how non-medical problems have become increasingly medicalised (Conrad, 2000). Zola (1972) suggested a process that 'mystifies the inter-relationship between the individual and the wider social and economic structures'. Individuals, in this sense, are becoming defined and labelled through depression constructs.

There are a number of life events that cause people distress but a key issue is the extent to which the unhappiness that results from this is tolerated or not. Unhappiness now is seen as depression, an emotion that is social in context rather than psychological (Middleton and Shaw, 2000). It is suggested that contemporary medical psychiatry has, in large, maintained its scientific view of mental illness to maintain its status within medicine. As a result, 'sadness has been re-named "depression" and becomes not a human emotion, brought on by the effects of complex social an personal inter-factors but, a pathology residing in a dysfunctional individual' (Riley, 1988: 26). What once existed as a human emotion has now become embroiled in diagnostic criteria. This authority and control of modern psychiatry is evident through the increasing everyday usage of psychiatric terminology. This implies that a normal human reaction to a given event can now be classified as a condition that is treatable by experts (Riley, 1998). In his famous polemic, Bental noted his surprise that happiness was not classified as a disorder:

> It is proposed that happiness be classified as a psychiatric disorder and be included in future editions of the major diagnostic manuals under the new name: major effective disorder, pleasant type.(Bentall, 1992: 94)

The increase in medical categories appears to support the notion that medicalisation is taking place. A key component here however is to what extent these categories are being developed through society's increasing demand for a quick fix to what is perceived by the individual as depression. Conrad (2000: 323) suggested 'the extent to which medicalisation is increasing is not simply a result of medical colonisation'. This is a pivotal point within the medicalisation debate. Evidence points to the idea that the (public's tolerance) for mild symptoms and benign problems has (decreased,)spurring a progressive medicalisation of physical distress.... (and we would add mental distress)' (Barksy and Borus, 2000: 323). The growth of medicalisation can occur [therefore] due to an increase in supply or demand for medical categorisation. Zola (1997) very much underpinned this concept through a further definition of medicalisation, which sees it as 'an insidious and undramatic phenomenon accomplished by "medicalising" much of daily living, by making labels "health" and "ill" relevant to an increasing part of human existence'.

It is further argued that the current classification system (DSM) for psychiatric disorders 'reflects a combination of public and professional attitudes towards the origins of deviant behaviour and how it would be controlled' (Tausig et al., 1999: 139). This only refers however to a small percentage of referrals from doctors to psychiatric services. If it is becoming more acceptable for new illnesses to become caught up and re-defined within the medical diagnostic criteria then the public at large are medicalising problems. Taken one step further, a process of individual medicalisation is taking place in conjunction with the medical response to increasing demand. This challenges the traditional view of the patient's vulnerability and powerlessness within their bargaining position with the GP. As society has become more adept at problem solving within the medical realm, so a discourse has developed in which health is seen as a basic human need, and medical care has become perceived as a social right. The importance placed on health and health care have been incorporated into our notion of human citizenship 'rights', the provision of which society will generally be held responsible (Butler, 1973). Health has become conceptualised as a fundamental, universal entitlement. The protection and maintenance of rights (such a health) are often accomplished through formalised systems – such as state-run health care. As our understanding of rights expands to encompass more of our daily lives, so the fundamental institution of the state have tended to expand their activities to meet those understandings (Giddens, 1998). Therefore, the right 'not to be unhappy' is beginning to emerge and this may account for the meteoric rise in the incidence of depression, not only in the UK but throughout Western Europe (Shaw and Middleton, 2001), with the result that unhappiness is becoming individually medicalised.

Manifestations in Primary Care

Figures 1 and 2, though based on data from the mid 1990s (Goldberg and Huxley, 1980), are useful in illustrating the extent of 'demand' from the general public for the treatment of depression and anxiety in primary care medical services. The community sample in Figure 1, based on OPCS (Meltzer, Pettigrew and Hinds, 1995), indicates that almost a third of the population regards themselves as having some form of mental distress, and that just under a quarter of the population seek medical assistance from their General Practitioner. Of those with a self perception of mental distress 79 per cent cite depression, anxiety or a mixture of both anxiety and depression as the descriptor of their problem. Subsequent research suggests that this information continues to be valid (Shaw and Middleton, 2000).

This demand places great strain upon primary care resources. As recently as 50 years ago depression, as we understand it, was rare (Healy, 1995). Today, patients with psycho/social distress represent around 30 per cent of all initial GP consultations, and around 50 per cent of consecutive attendances at a GPs surgery (Kessler et al., Gray 1999). A further point to notice from figure 1 is that almost two thirds of those attending GPs surgeries do not have their self-diagnosis ratified by the GP. They are recognised as distressed but the GP does not regard that distress as illness. Even so GPs are under a high degree of criticism from Psychiatry over medicalising social distress and the high rates of 'inappropriate' referrals from primary care to psychiatry and high rates of benzodiazepine prescribing (Middleton and Shaw, 2000). The majority of patients identified as depressed in primary care do not necessarily display signs of a formally defined mental illness. It has consequently been suggested that many are distressed rather than ill (Shaw and Middleton, 2001). Of course, treating distress as mental illness in a primary care environment would constitute the medicalisation of a normal human response to adverse life events.

This does pose a number of questions relating to the diagnosis of depression and this has encouraged a number of further studies, considering aspects of the diagnostic process (Chew-Graham et al., 2001; Shaw and Middleton, 2001; Howe, 1996). Studies have explored GPs' perceptions and ability to detect psychological distress, patient's views concerning their own health, and the relationship between diagnosis of depression at primary care level and inappropriate referral letters to psychiatric services. GPs respond with arguments about a non-appreciation of the context of pressure on diagnosis in the primary care setting (Shaw and Middleton 2001; Chew-Graham et al., 2001).

It is consequently worth first exploring the notion that the population is self medicalising their problems and why this may be the case, before moving on to examine the context in which the GPs may be 'inappropriately' accepting offers of illness from the public – thus medicalising.

The Medicalisation of Daily Living

A starting point for much of medical sociology is that illness is a form of deviance. As such, notions about illness have to be related to some concept of normal 'health'. This norm is socially constructed and will vary from culture to culture and over historical time (Pilgrim and Bental, 1999). It could be argued that in Western society misery is being seen not only as deviant to social norms, but also a part of the preserve of medicine.

We would argue that high rates of medicalisation are actually indicative of systemic problems in western society. T.S. Eliot (1936) wrote 'What life have you if not life together? There is no life that is not in community …'. Community is where individuals are recognised and their individuality affirmed. Community is also the place of support mechanisms. The relevance of the traditional anchors and support mechanisms of community – the family, neighbourhood and the church have been sharply eroded over the last 50 years in the UK. In its place is a consumer culture centred on the fulfilment of individual desires and where the individual has become the core unit of social consumption.

One of the vehicles for this change is the consumer culture. The sociological study of consumption is bound up with notions of what it is to be a fully developed human being, morally and spiritually (Shaw and Aldridge, 2002; Aldridge, 2003). Shaw and Aldridge (2002) use Maslow's argument that human motivation across all societies, and at all times, is organised in a hierarchical structure of need to focus upon the value of consumer society. As each lower level of need is met, so the next higher level comes into force. Maslow's 'need hierarchy' has seven levels, which in descending order are:

Self-actualisation needs
Aesthetic needs
Cognitive needs
Esteem needs
Belonging, love and esteem needs
Safety needs
Physiological needs

One way to read Maslow's need hierarchy is as a ladder on which we climb from 'animalism' to humanity and one way of stating the limitations of consumer society is to say that it can satisfy only our animal needs.

Consumerism can meet our physiological need for nutrition and our safety need for shelter. By the time we reach the third and fourth levels - belonging, love and esteem – consumerism, like Mephistopheles, delivers the semblance but not the substance. We may try to purchase love, friendship and respect, but what we buy will be prostitutes, parasites and toadies. At levels five and six - our cognitive need for knowledge and understanding and our aesthetic need for beauty - consumerism is a spent force. As for self-actualisation, the fulfilment of our potential as human beings, consumerism is its antithesis. Consumerism does not raise us up, it drags us down. (Shaw & Aldridge, 2002: 10)

Another strand in thinking about consumerism and what it is to be human derives from the ethical writings of Aristotle. Aristotle's influence runs powerfully through the analysis of the poverty of contemporary moral philosophy, and in the discussion of the processes by which character has been corroded by changes in the world of work. Scruton (1998) argues in Aristotelian fashion that we must not confuse pleasure and happiness. Pleasure results from satisfying desires, but happiness comes through fulfilment as a person. Pleasure is precarious because it depends on good luck, but happiness is robust because it flows from virtue. Shaw and Aldridge (2002) argue that consumption delivers only pleasure, not happiness. However, happiness, not pleasure, is the final goal of human life, and only through living as much for others as for oneself can people really be happy and reach their full potential (which is self-actualisation).

Contemporary consumer society certainly seems to possess a diminished capacity to answer the question of 'who we are'. Fukuyama (2000) argued that the quest for identity, recognition and happiness is 'one of the chief motors of the entire human historical process'. In a competitive individualistic society, which is hierarchical, the 'appearance of being socially denigrated or humiliated endangers the identity of human beings, just as infection with disease endangers their physical life' (Honneth, 1995). This is leading to demands for 'the right to be esteemed and recognised', particularly for those feeling vulnerable in a competitive individualistic society. As Furedi writes:

> The belief that the defining feature of the self is its vulnerability informs Anglo-American cultures ethnopsychology. In this context recognition of the self implies recognising the condition and experience of vulnerability... For the individual, the disclosure of vulnerability has the status of a moral statement that invites social and cultural affirmation. It encourages the 'establishment of suffering as a measure of social virtue'. That is why it has become common for many people to define themselves through a psychological or medical diagnosis. Even behind the cultural demand for recognition lurks this therapeutic imperative. (Furedi, 2002: 5)

The rise of 'therapeutic demand' arising from a breakdown of solidarity and community is becoming manifest in a number of areas. For example, Wainwright and Calnan have recently researched work stress and have argued that the massive increase in work-related stress is related to the breakdown of trade unionism and collective means of solving work-related problems. As trade unionism becomes unacceptable problems have been expressed through a bio-medical idiom (Wainwright and Calnan, 2002). As Furedi (2002: 6) points out 'since the 1980s a more individuated workplace ethos has fostered a climate where problems are readily medicalised. At a time of existential insecurity, a medical diagnosis at least has the virtue of definition'. A disease both explains an individual's behaviour and helps to ratify a sense of identity. In other words, the medicalisation of everyday life allows individuals to make sense of their predicament and gain moral sympathy. It could also be argued to represent a socially sanctioned claim for recognition. As a consequence, there is a demand from people to expand diagnosis in medicine to recognise their situation (eg ME, Attention Deficit Disorder, Gulf War Syndrome, Post Traumatic Stress Disorder, RSI etc). In doing this, people are 'relieved of responsibility' for their behaviour as they gain recognition for their situation. It is a search for identity and a valorisation of a person's individual difference through the claim for therapeutic status - because therapy is seen as a vehicle to social affirmation. The argument is that some people are driven by a deep psychological need to be recognised and affirmed, and so seek identity and recognition in this way because they cannot achieve it in a competitive individualistic society. Ironically, as Fuerdi (2002: 7) points out, 'their identity then becomes attached to its own social exclusion because it is attached to social exclusion for its very existence as identity'.

Certainly, many GPs in a recent study (Shaw, 2003) stated that patients were looking for a 'quick fix' or a 'magic bullet' or pill that would make them happy. This is also the background to the massive growth of the 'psy-industries' of counselling and psychotherapy, as the traditional coping mechanisms of the community have been eroded. People are 'buying into' such services in search of happiness and self-fulfilment, but such services can only reconcile people to 'what is' and in doing so also renders self-identity dependent upon those professionals.

Responding to Demand: The Role of General Practitioners

The extent of the demands made upon GPs that arise from drives for recognition has been mentioned and is evident in Figure 1. The notion of patients actually seeking the medicalisation of their emotional and/or personal problems has often been constructed by GPs in terms of a social aetiology. Patients presenting at GPs surgeries were derived from their knowledge that there is an illness called depression, that it seems widespread, and that doctors are there to treat it. This is informed by the media and what people see happens to people around them – in terms of receiving treatment. As an example, a very popular TV soap in the UK called 'EastEnders' saw one of the principal characters go to see her GP because she was unhappy the day after her fiancé left her, to come away with a prescription for Prozac. Such things inform public perceptions of the level of unhappiness for which it is appropriate to seek assistance from the GP. To quote from a GP cited in a recent study by Chew-Graham (2002), (which echoed the findings cited earlier):

— *Reference?*

Patients actually a lot of the time want a medical answer. They want a quick fix, they want to have something done.

In terms of ideology, patients want to know (and want others to know) that it is the illness (depression) that is at fault rather than them and that they are undertaking a course of treatment. This is a view reinforced by David Healy in his work on entitled 'The Antidepressant Era' (1995). Shaw (2002) highlighted the strategies that patients use to try and control a consultation and direct it towards their desired end. This illustrates the negotiated nature of diagnosis. Patient strategies include rehearsal, partly presenting or expanding symptoms, excluding information and ignoring doctors' advice.

GPs in an initial consultation typically have only between 7 and 10 minutes to make a diagnosis and decide upon a treatment. The officially recognised diagnostic criteria for depression are contained in ISD 10 and DSM 4. These are weighty tomes which are not of much use in the context of a 10 minute consultation. There is also evidence that they are not used in the context of a 45 minute psychiatric assessment (Middleton, 2002).

Furthermore, linking to Shaw's (2002) work, one of the benefits to patients of adopting expert knowledge systems is that they are best able to communicate with professionals. Work by Abbott has highlighted the ways in which people 'preprofessionalise' their thinking and language in the lead up to an encounter with a professional. They do this in order to present their case in the best possible light (Abbott, 1988). Equally, of course, clinical tasks are embedded in the social process of authoring the accounts of patients' symptoms to fit medical categories (Clark and Mishler, 1992).

In the context of high caseloads and associated severe problems with GP recruitment, depression is conceptualised as an everyday problem of managing workload in a practice rather than an objective diagnostic category (Chew-Graham, 2000). What is clear is that patients who get what they want out of a consultation are likely to leave the surgery quickly. Given the high levels of demand upon the GPs to treat psycho-social distress and the work and diagnostic context it seems almost inevitable that some degree of medicalisation will occur at this level, despite the fact that GPs are clearly attempting to reduce the numbers of people they treat and are engaging in their traditional gate-keeping role.

The Diagnosis of Depression in Primary Care

A recent interview study undertaken by Shaw (2002) has illustrated that the criteria for diagnosis of depression in primary care is quite wide:

> For me the key points are chronic low mood for at least two weeks, anhedonia (absence of pleasure), biological symptoms and social dysfunction. Of these I place a lot of evidence on anhedonia. 'Is there anything pleasurable in your life?' or 'Are you looking forward to anything' are useful questions in helping to determine whether someone is simply sad or miserable from someone who is depressed. (GP1)

> Older GPs may be more likely to base their diagnosis upon 'judgement' and all GPs may sometimes treat 'depression' even if the patient would only fulfil the criteria for 'minor depression' (essentially low mood with less than four characteristics). (GP2)

However, it is not so much the diagnosis as the image of 'doctor as helper' that may inform the analysis:

> When we feel powerless to help the patient in any other way or we can see that they have no other resource to turn to, then sometimes it is easy to read into a situation the diagnosis of depression (GP3)

These quotes and the wider interview study picked up on two key points informing diagnosis:

1. Diagnosis both accommodates and acknowledges the reality of existential despair that is framed as a key component of depression by patients. GPs may see someone living in deprived circumstances, with gangs of youths roaming around outside the patient's door, cramped living conditions with damp running down the walls – they can do little about the context, but they can relieve the misery by prescribing antidepressants.

2. Conceptions of health and illness reflect the values of capitalism and individualism, in that they are imbued with notions of self-discipline, self-denial, self-control and willpower. 'The moral prescription (or norm) of a healthy life was found to be a cheerful stoicism evident in the refusal to worry, or to complain or to be morbid' (Cornwell, 1984). Notions of dependency in Western societies are regarded as negative. Having the strength to overcome problems reflects more general social norms and values found in capitalist societies.

It is certainly the case that an ideology of 'robust individualism', which stresses the individual's right to lead a satisfying life, is coming more into the publics (un) consciousness.

Linking back to a point made earlier by Furedi (2002) on the dependency which can arise in people seeking recognition through diagnosis, May and Kelly (1982) have highlighted the problems which can arise once the diagnosis is made:

> Paradoxically once the definition of mental ill health has been made, the patient begins to acquire a particularly vested interest in sustaining the definition. By confirming or giving definition to the lay diagnosis the doctor transfers 'blame' for the patients present status and behaviour to the 'condition' and the responsibility for care onto himself... in all of this the patient is by no means passive. Having an illness absolves him from responsibility and entitles him to care; despite the stigma there is power here. Being mentally ill is a status, which paradoxically confers the power to control family and friends and doctors and treatment agents. (May and Kelly, 1992)

In Conclusion

The politics of recognition linked with the increasing medical understanding of lay people has led to the medicalisation of everyday life. As some people search for recognition in a society, which they think does not care about them, they are seeking diagnosis and therapy as a means to social affirmation. This leads to increasing demands upon primary care practitioners, especially GPs. The traditional power imbalance between GPs and their patients appears to have changed. It no longer seems to be GPs medicalising problems but rather an attempt to manage demand. It could be argued that they could be more efficient in 'sifting out' the social from the medical. However, this must be seen in the context of the pressures of work, the difficulty of making a diagnosis of a complex condition in a very short time frame, and the marketing of antidepressants which are increasingly targeted at milder and milder forms of 'depression' for profitability. The demands on GPs result from individual solutions to systemic problems. And it is consequently at the level of social change that the solution to demands should lie.

Figure 1 Incidence of 'Mental Illness'

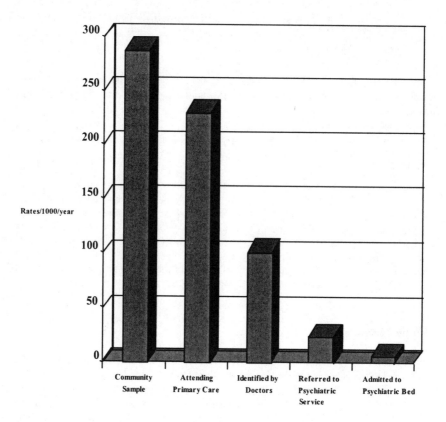

References

Abbott, A. (1988), *The System of Professions: An Essay on the Division of Expert Labour*, Chicago: Chicago University Press.

Aldridge, A. (2003), *Consumption*, Cambridge, Polity Press.

Bentall, R.P. (1992) 'A proposal to classify happiness as a psychiatric disorder', *Journal of Medical Ethics*, 18: 94-98 1992.

Butler, J.R. (1973), *Family Doctors and Public Policy: a Study of Manpower Re-distribution*, London: Routledge and Kegan Paul.

Chew-Graham, C.A., May, C.R., Cole, H. and Hedley, S. (2001), 'The burden of depression in primary care: a qualitative investigation of general practitioners' constructs of depressed people in inner city', *Primary Care Psychiatry*, 6: 4.

Conrad, P. (ed.) (1997), *The Sociology of Health and Illness: Critical Perspectives*, New York: St. Martins Press.

Conrad, P. (2000), *Medicalisation, Generticas, and Human Problems, Handbook of Medical Sociolog*, 5th Edition pp. 322-333.

Eaton, W.W. (2001), *The Sociology of Mental Disorders*, Westport CT: Praeger.

Eliot, T.S (1936), 'Choruses from The Rock', *Collected Poems 1909-1935*, Faber and Faber.

Forde, R. (1996), 'Inclusion of Psychosocial Conditions in Clinical Practice and the Problem of Medicalisation', *Theoretical Medicine*, 17: 151-161.

Fox, R.C. (1997), 'The Medicalization and Demedicalization of American Society', in Conrad, P. (ed.) (1997), *The Sociology of Health and Illness: Critical Perspectives*, New York: St. Martins Press.

Friedson, E. (1988), 'The formal characteristics of a profession', in *Profession of Medicine: A Study of the Sociology of Applied Knowledge*, Chicago, Ill: University of Chicago Press: 71-84.

Freidson, E. (1970), *Profession of Medicine*, New York: Dodd, Mead.

Fukuyama, F. (2000), 'The Great Disruption: Human nature and the reconstitution of social order', Touchstone: New York.

Furedi, F. (2002), 'The Institutionalisation of Recognition – Evaluating the Moral Stalemate', paper presented to DMAP Conference, University of Cardiff, 4-6th April.

Giddens, A. (1998), *The Third Way*, Cambridge: Polity Press.

Goldberg, D and Huxley, P. (1980), *Mental Illness in the Community: the Pathway to Psychiatric Care,*. London: Tavistock Press, 1980.

Hafferty, F. and McKinlay, J. (eds) (1993), *The Changing Medical Profession: an International Perspective*, Oxford: Oxford University Press.

Healy, D. (1997), *The Anti-Depressant Era*, Cambridge (Mass): Harvard University Press.

Honneth, A. (1995), *The Struggle for Recognition: The Moral Grammar of Social Conflicts*, Cambridge: Polity Press.

Howe, A. (1996), 'I know what to do, but it's not possible to do it – general practitioners' perceptions of their ability to detect psychological distress', *Family Practice*, Oxford University Press.

Illch, I. (1975), *Medical Nemesis, the Exploration of Health*, Calder & Boyars.

Kessler, D, Lloyd, K, Lewis, G and Pereira Gray, D. (1999), 'Cross sectional study of symptom attribution and recognition of depression and anxiety in primary care', *BMJ*; 318: 436-439.

Lyon, M. (1996), 'C. Wright Mills meets Prozac: the relevance of 'social emotion' to the sociology of health and illness', in James, V. and Gabe, J. (eds) *Health and the Sociology of Emotions*, Blackwell.

Meltzer, H., Gill, B., Pettigrew, M. and Hinds, K. (1995), *The Prevalence of Psychiatric Morbidity amongst Adults Living in Private Households*, London: HMSO, 1995.

Middleton, H. and Shaw, I. (2000), 'Distinguishing mental illness in primary care', *British Medical Journal*, vol. 320, pp. 320-321.

Panorama (13th May 2001), The Tranquilliser Trap, BBC1.

Peterson, A. and Bunton, R. (eds) (1997), *Foucault: Health and Illness*, Routledge.

Pilgrim, D. and Bentall, R (1999), 'The Medicalisation of Misery: A critical realist analysis of the concept of depression', *Journal of Mental Health*, 8: 3: 261-271.

Pitts, J. (1968), 'Social control: the concept', *International Encyclopaedia of Social Sciences*, Vol. 14, New York: Macmillan

Riley, M. (1998), 'Understanding depression, insight', *Nursing Times*, 94: 44.

Rose, N. (1986), *The Power of Psychiatry*, in Miller, P. and Rose, N. (eds), Polity Press: Oxford.

Rosen, G. (1972), 'The evolution of social medicine', in Howard E. Freeman, Sol Levine, and Leo Reeder, *Handbook of Medical Sociology*, pp. 30-60, Englewood Cliffs, New Jersey: Prentice Hall.

Shaw, I. (2002), 'How lay are lay beliefs?', *Health*, vol.6 (3), pp. 287-299.

Shaw, I., (2003), 'Doctors, Dirty Work and "Revolving Doors"', paper submitted to *Qualitative Health Research* (currently under review).

Shaw, I. and Aldridge A. (2002), 'Consumerism, unhappiness and the role of medicine in society', *Leaves*; the magazine of the Southwell Minster Community, August 2002, 9-10

Shaw, I. and Middleton, H. (2001), 'Recognising depression in primary care', *The Journal of Primary Care Mental Health*, 5:2.

Szasz, T. (1970), *Ideology and Insanity: Essays on the Psychiatric Dehumanisation of Man*, Garden City, NY: Doubleday.

Tausig, M., Michello, J. and Subed, S. (1999), *A Sociology of Mental Illness*, Prentice Hall: USA.

Tucket, D. and Kaufert, J.M. (eds) (1978), *Basic Readings in Medical Sociology*.

Wainwright, D. and Calnan, M. (2002), *Work Stress*, Open University Press.

Zola, I (1972), 'Medicine as an institution of social control', *Sociological Review*, 20:487-504

Zola, I. (1997), 'Medicine as an institution of social control', in Conrad, P. (ed.) *The Sociology of Health and Illness: Critical Perspectives*, New York: St. Martins Press.

Zola, I. (1999), 'Medicalization as a problem for preventative medicine', *Biothics*, 13:2.

Index